DANNY SILK

T0095806

UNPUNISHABLE

ENDING OUR LOVE AFFAIR WITH PUNISHMENT

FOREWORD BY SHAWN BOLZ

Unpunishable
Ending Our Love Affair With Punishment

ISBN: 978-1-947165-76-2

Printed in the United States
lovingonpurpose.com

To all the people I've worked with through the years who have been faithful to dig deep into humility and receive the grace of God that gives the power and desire to do His will.

ACKNOWLEDGEMENTS

Allison Armerding—Once again, you've pulled together another masterpiece! You are such a stellar human and a wonderful genius to work with. My gratitude goes beyond simple words. You are my friend.

Loving On Purpose Team—Sheri Silk, Ben and Brittney Serpell, Leah Rivas, Anna Hill, Ashley Beck, and Phin (Office Mascot, Golden Doodle). You all live this message so beautifully and are faithful representatives to the world that is watching and learning from you. Thank you for making this journey that much more fun and enjoyable.

Ryan Sprenger—Here we go again! Another "self-published" book that NewType and Printopya pulled together. I am so grateful for your leadership and servant heart. Thank you to you and your team!

Ben and Heather Armstrong—You are love champions and my personal heroes! I am challenged by the fruit of your lives. You have changed the course of history by simply saying, "I choose you."

Josh and Robin Biddlecomb—You are legends in my heart! Thank you for putting in those hard miles to reach the top of family legacy, and for trusting God to work all things together for good.

Pep and Angie Robey—You sure changed my life with your story. I am forever grateful for your courage and reconciliation.

Jonathon and Karen Welton—Thank you for your help with this book! From theology to humility, you are both major contributors to the "better covenant" on the earth. I am happy to walk with you and to call you friends.

Dann Farrelly—Thank you, once again, for the "plumb line" and the strength you have added to my life.

Shawn Bolz—Your friend heart runs deep! I love what I see you building in this life. Cherie was a classy move, as are the lovely ladies you've added to the household. Thanks for your help with this project!

TABLE OF CONTENTS

FOREWORD

I was raised by two first-generation Christians who had lived broken lives before coming to Christ. They grew up in very broken families where there had been abuse, anger, and punishment. My parents were also children of the 1950s and raised their kids from the '60s to the '80s, so the parenting role models, both in popular psychology and the church, were punishment-based. My parents knew they didn't want to parent me and my siblings the way they were parented, however, and fought to learn how to keep connection with us and not risk losing it by being overly harsh with us. They did an amazing job of working through their salvation right in front of us.

I remember one time, my dad was so angry when I had done something wrong that he looked at me and said, "I shouldn't be this angry. What you have done doesn't deserve this kind of response. I don't want you to feel like my anger is your responsibility to manage or is related to what you have done. Why don't you go play while I work on calming down and managing my anger with God so that I can talk to you about what you have done in a right way."

My dad's self-awareness spared me from feeling wrath in a situation where so many experience harsh judgment, punishment, and consequences instead of real love, connection, and commitment. His vulnerability showed me what his goals were when I did something wrong. It wasn't to express himself—it was to help me understand that he was a real human recovering from real brokenness caused by his own parents, who had used control and anger to manage him. He didn't want to repeat that, and as his relationship with God grew, he became a good model to me and my sisters of being adaptable and setting new goals that were not based on the punishment model he had received. My parents both strived to live out something different in their Christianity, which seemed rare in the culture of the time and made our family unique.

The fruit of their transition from a punishment model to a discipline model led to my sisters and me barely experiencing any real self-inflicted trouble in our lives. I have never been drunk, tried drugs, had premarital sex, or done anything illegal—not because I was afraid of the punishment of my parents or the law, but because the way my parents showed me God's love and their love caused me to want to protect that connection at all costs. My dad modeled what it looked like to *not* chase other women or have a pornography habit from the time I was young, because he loved my mom so much he didn't want to lose any of that connection. It caused me to believe that if I hurt my connections with them, which I did a few times in real ways, I would need to fight for repentance, reconciliation, and connection at all costs.

When I sat down to read the manuscript for this book, I was expecting a good read, but I was also busy, so I was telling myself, "Be really present and connected with this." Boy, did I not need the self-talk. I was captured from the opening pages. I found myself stretched—in a good way, but also almost uncomfortably—first through the stories, then through Danny's language for approaching one of the most difficult subjects in Christianity: How do we walk out the painful parts of our relational journey and see them through a biblical lens? How do we do repentance? How do we build reconciliation? How do walk out healthy conflict with people like our children or others we lead or are responsible for? Also, when *we* sin, how do we walk out rebuilding connection and setting the goals for repentance, as opposed to just working out of shame and guilt? How do we not punish each other or ourselves?

In Christianity, we have lacked emotional *and* spiritual intelligence across the board for knowing what to do when someone fails us and themselves. We know we are supposed to live the radical life of love Jesus modeled for us. Yet, punishment is humanity's go-to, and so many times we end up defaulting to self-protection and harsh discipline instead of love-based discipline, and we put ourselves or others in a position where we just can't succeed. When you read *Unpunishable*, you will unlearn and learn some important things as you are confronted by the simple, biblical response we are called to have toward sin and failure, as well as how to have a heart response to people in your life and in our culture.

This book is giving me new spiritual intelligence to deal with failure. I immediately started to see the stakes differently in relationship. I also had to rethink some of the interactions I have had with friends, family, employees, and church members in the past because I didn't always live out of a healthy theology or have language to define it. I am doing some soul-searching to recover anything I have lost because of the times I have acted from a punishment mindset instead of the mindset of grace and reconciliation that Danny so clearly expresses in *Unpunishable*. That's just how honest I have to be in writing this foreword. This book will make you change. It will set a new structure inside of you—a new response to sin, repentance, conflict, and a process around these issues. I think almost everyone who reads this will have quick, visible growth in some areas that are so misunderstood in the church today. Ultimately, *Unpunishable* is a revolution of theology that is love-based, approachable, spiritually intelligent, and clean.

I was sitting with Danny several years ago and gave him a spiritual word: "You are going to write a book about leaders and people who have failed, and you are going to give language for what the process of restoration really looks like and how to deal with repentance and reconciliation." He would have done it with or without my spiritual input, because this is who God is through Danny, but I needed this book and am glad that I was spiritually aware enough to want it. I am being transformed by this book, and so will you.

Shawn Bolz

Author of *Through the Eyes of Love, Translating God, Breakthrough Prayers, Prophecies, and Declarations*

TV and PODCAST host of Translating God on TBN and Exploring the Prophetic Podcast

SECTION I

OUR LOVE AFFAIR WITH PUNISHMENT

CHAPTER 1

THE CHOICE TO REPENT

It was the second day of our Culture of Honor leadership conference at Bethel Church. Before me sat around two hundred leaders, many of whom were looking at me curiously, clearly unsure what to expect from this afternoon session, which was simply titled "Unpunishable." As for me, I was anticipating that for many of those leaders, what was about to happen would drop a small spiritual nuke into their worlds.

"Over the last few sessions," I began, "We've explored the idea that a culture of honor is a culture of love and a culture of family. This means that it is also a culture of vulnerability. We are choosing to position ourselves in relationships where our lives can be powerfully impacted by the choices of other people, and they can be impacted by our choices. And sometimes, the impact of those choices is extremely painful. This is why most of the world sacrifices genuine love and community for the sake of self-protection. But in a culture of honor, in a family, we sacrifice self-protection to pursue connection when it's been damaged or destroyed by someone's poor choice."

A few heads nodded around the room, but most of the faces looking at me were sober and attentive. Everyone seemed to sense that we were wading out into weighty waters.

"The best way to show you what this honor, love, and vulnerability look like," I continued, "is with a story—a story about one of our leaders who made a painful choice that affected everyone in our environment."

"One day in 2009," I began, "Dann Farrelly, one of our senior leaders, and I were called into a meeting with one of our ministry school interns. This intern explained to us that she had been living with one of the school pastors and his family for a year, and that over the previous several months, she had become involved in an affair with him."

On cue, a taut silence filled the room, a silence that remained as I went on with the story.

Dann and I had wasted no time in calling a meeting to confront the pastor in question, Ben Armstrong. He admitted that everything she had told us was the truth. He seemed to be shocked by his own confession—it was clearly the first time he'd said out loud what he'd actually been doing.

Such confessions are always heartbreaking to hear, but this one was especially saddening, because I knew this man well. In fact, I had known Ben since he was a boy growing up in my hometown, Weaverville, California. He, his wife, Heather, and their three children were beloved members of our Bethel community. Ben had risen steadily through the ranks of Bethel's staff, to the point where we had entrusted him with the direct pastoral care of seventy first-year students and oversight of the (then) seven-hundred-member first-year class. His sphere of influence included the school, church, and even our extended church network. His choice to violate his marriage covenant also violated his covenants with God and all the people of God who trusted him as a leader.

When I reached this point in the story—Ben's confession—I stopped and asked the room of leaders to write down the answers to two questions:

- *What are you feeling and thinking about Ben and his choice?*
- *If this situation was happening in your life or area of responsibility, what would you do next?*

A RANGE OF REACTIONS

As I gave the leaders a few minutes to write their responses, I scanned the audience, wondering what was going on in the hearts and minds of these men and women. Certain individuals stood out to me, and I couldn't resist forming hunches about some of the reactions they were likely experiencing, based on what I knew of their stories.

The first person I noticed was Chuck,[1] who I'd only just met a few hours earlier during lunch. Chuck had told me that this was his first visit to Bethel. His new pastor had been introducing "revival culture" at their conservative evangelical church in the Midwest and had brought Chuck and a handful of other volunteer leaders to this conference to experience firsthand what he'd been guiding them towards. Chuck had also mentioned to me that he had an eighteen-year-old daughter who was considering applying for the school of ministry after she graduated from high school.

By the look of his clenched jaw and narrowed eyes, I suspected that the dominant emotion Chuck was experiencing in reaction to Ben's story was anger. I'd seen that look many times. It was the look of a man thinking something like, *If some pastor seduced my daughter, I would hunt him down and shoot him! How could someone in a trusted position of power take advantage of someone like that? I hope they made an example of him. He certainly should never be allowed in any kind of church leadership position again!*

---

[1] Names and details of the leaders in this section have been changed to protect their identities.

The next person who caught my eye was Alexandra, a lay leader at a church in Idaho. I had met her several months earlier at another Bethel conference, and on that occasion her glowing face and ecstatic descriptions of what she'd been experiencing were filled with a starry-eyed hope that she'd discovered a church that, as far as she could tell, was pretty close to perfect. Now, her face had fallen into lines of disappointment. I could almost hear her thinking, *Wow. I thought this was a place where people really lived out the will of God "on earth as it is in heaven." I thought the leaders here had it more together. A pastor having an affair with his intern? How could he be living in the middle of revival and mess up like that?*

At the table next to Alexandra sat a group of leaders from Singapore. My eyes zeroed in on Li, a leader I'd spent a fair amount of time with on several ministry trips to Asia. In all our conversations about the kinds of leadership challenges he faced in his culture, sexual misconduct had not come up as a major issue and was apparently rarely heard of among their Christian leaders. The stiff, serious look on Li's face suggested that he was feeling righteous indignation that a minister of the gospel would behave in such a shameful manner. Based on what I understood of his culture, I knew he would probably advocate strict punishment to send the message to everyone that such behavior was deplorable for anyone, especially a pastor.

At the back of the room, I spotted my friend Walter, a fifty-year-old businessman and lifelong believer from Tulsa, Oklahoma. After the opening session of the conference the previous day, we'd spent some time catching up together, and Walter had shared that he'd just been through a very tough betrayal. He'd recently discovered that his brother-in-law, who he'd hired two years before after he was fired from another job, was claiming false expenses and writing company checks to himself. Walter hadn't pressed charges, but he had told his brother-in-law that it was time for him to find another job. "It broke my heart," he'd told me, "but I had to let him face the consequences of his behavior. My only hope is that he learns his lesson and never hurts people like this again." I could easily imagine Walter would think something similar should be done in Ben's case.

Also sitting near the back was a long-time ministry acquaintance, Carolyn, her face suffused with anxiety that I knew had less to do with Ben's story than with a situation in her personal life. In the years I'd known Carolyn and her husband Ken, they'd always been a model Christian family, raising their three beautiful daughters in the church where Carolyn had worked as bookkeeper for eleven years. The girls were very involved in youth group and Ken was on the board of elders. But now, something was threatening to turn their world upside down. At lunch the day before, Carolyn had pulled my wife Sheri aside and confided that just that week, she and Ken had learned that their middle daughter, who was barely fifteen, was pregnant. She hadn't yet told their pastor the news and had asked Sheri for advice on what to do. She was convinced that when the leadership and congregation knew how she had failed as a parent, they would want to remove her from her role in the church administration so she wouldn't reflect poorly on the senior pastor. Based on her expression, I suspected that hearing Ben's story could only be aggravating the fear of punishment she was currently dealing with.

The last person who caught my eye was a pastor friend of mine, Bruce, who was sitting at a table with three new members of his elder team. The three young guys had their heads together at the table and were showing one another what they had written down on their papers. Bruce, however, was turned away from them and seemed to be avoiding eye contact. He looked . . . uncomfortable. In ten-plus years of connecting and ministering together at various events, Bruce and I had shared enough of our stories for me to know that he had struggled with a porn problem in the past. Based on some of the stressful situations I knew he was currently dealing with in his congregation, I couldn't help wonder if Bruce was struggling in that area again. If so, it would explain why hearing about a pastor being caught and exposed had him shifting in his seat.

FINDING THE PROBLEM

Once everyone had finished writing, I said, "So at this point in the conversation, I had Ben's confession. In most cases, that's where the conversation stops. That's where we start to tell someone who has broken one of the sacred rules of the community what is going to happen next. The message we send is that they have no more choices to be made in this process. But from my perspective, Ben still had one choice to make—the most important choice of all. Would he repent or not?"

This time, I didn't see any nods in the audience. Many, including Chuck and Walter, looked incredulous, as if to say, *Why would that matter?* Others looked confused and uncertain, seemingly unsure of what I meant by "repent."

"The first way for me to determine whether Ben was repentant," I continued, "was to find out if he was willing to really look at the mess he had made. He had admitted to the behavior, but that was only part of the picture. To repent, he needed to see the whole problem—the internal core beliefs and motives that had produced the behavior, and all of its effects."

I went on to describe the next stage of our conversation with Ben, which started with me asking him, "So what happened, Ben? How would you let something like this into your life?"

By now, Ben's look of post-confession shock had already been replaced by deep sighs and tears of fear, guilt, and remorse. I was pretty sure he didn't need to be convinced he had a problem—he knew he was in the biggest trouble of his life. But instead of running out of the room, he began to search with us for the source of where things had gone wrong for him, and why.

After piecing together the events, decisions, and relational dynamics that had led to the affair, Ben saw the reality of the life he'd been living.

Not only had he been disconnected from his wife for years, he had been almost completely isolated from everyone around him. The husband, father, leader, and man he presented was a front—nobody really knew him or saw what was going on behind the curtain.

When I asked Ben what was driving these patterns of disconnection, isolation, and hiding in his life, it took him several minutes of hard thinking to identify the truth. Finally, he came out with, "I'm afraid of being seen and known because I'm afraid of doing something wrong and being punished."

"Okay," I said. "Let's go after that. Where do you think that fear is coming from?"

Ben mentioned a few "getting in trouble" scenarios from his childhood, but we hit pay dirt when he made another confession. This wasn't his first affair. He had committed adultery once twelve years before, when he and Heather were newly married and expecting their first child. At the time, he had been on staff at a small church. When the truth came out, he had gone through a "church discipline" process. First, he'd been required to go before the church congregation and confess what he had done. Then he had been relieved of all his leadership duties but was allowed to remain on staff as the church custodian. The only people with whom he had permission to discuss the situation were the senior pastors, who were supposed to counsel him and Heather, though in actuality, very little counseling took place. He and Heather had agreed to sweep the whole thing under the rug and move forward like nothing had happened. Eventually, the church leaders decided that Ben had "served his time" as the custodian, and he was gradually allowed to resume his pastoring duties.

When we hired Ben, we knew nothing about this episode in his life, so we had never thought to set up any accountability for him or ask good questions like, "Is having a young lady living in your house a good idea or not?" And so, the road had been left wide open for Ben's fear of punishment to drive him into realizing the very thing he was afraid of. It was simply a matter of time before the misery of unresolved pain in his marriage and hiddenness from people around him became greater than his fear of being caught and punished, and he acted out in an illegitimate way to find connection just like he'd done twelve years before.

Once I sensed that Ben saw the internal picture of his mess, I shifted my questions to the external picture. I wanted him to understand what was at stake here. This wasn't just about his marriage or his job or even Bethel Church and the ministry school. It wasn't just about violating God's commandments. It was about a family—a family we both belonged to and were responsible to protect.

"Tell me—who is affected by this decision?" I asked.

One by one, Ben named the people he'd hurt with this betrayal. Heather. Their children. Their parents and extended family. His intern. His staff team. The other revival group pastors and church leadership. His revival group. All the first-year students. The second-year students too—especially those who had been in his revival group the previous year. As the size of the mess came into staggering focus, Ben began to sob with grief.

Ben's tears were certainly appropriate, and his brokenness seemed real. He'd been willing to dig deep, answer my questions, and uncover the anatomy of his mess in full. Now he appeared to be experiencing the godly sorrow leading to repentance. But his answer to my final question would prove what was really in his heart.

"So, Ben . . . what are you going to do?" I asked.

Ben sat there for a moment, overwhelmed in the wake of the emotional tsunami that had just rolled through him. "I don't know," he said at last. "I know I need to try to clean up my mess. But I have no idea how. I feel pretty sure that I've just lost everything important in my life."

"Well, I can tell you that we will be behind you cleaning up your mess," I responded. "I can't tell you what everyone else will decide or what will happen. But I have seen situations like this turn around. It's going to work out better than you think."

A REPENTANCE JOURNEY

"Ben was repentant," I said to the room of leaders, "and that changed everything. But instead of telling you what happened next, I want to invite Ben and Heather to take over the story from here." I held out my hand toward the door of the conference room and beckoned.

In unison, every head whipped around and followed Ben and Heather as they entered the room and made their way, hand in hand, up the aisle to the front. When they reached me, I handed Ben the microphone.

"So, what was I going to do?" Ben began without preamble. "Like Danny said, I felt like my life was over and I had one option—to clean up my mess as best I could with every person I had betrayed. I had no idea how to do that or how it would pan out. I hadn't seen it mapped out in church, and I hadn't seen a success story, except maybe David in the Bible. But I discussed some ideas with Dann and Danny, and they agreed to be part of my support and accountability through the process. Then I began meeting with people, starting with Heather."

Ben and Heather tag-teamed in sharing the story of how Ben had confessed his sin to her after the confrontation meeting. He had gone home, called his parents, and asked them to come pick up the kids so he could talk to Heather. After hearing him out, she threw her wedding ring at him and told him to go get the kids so she could have some time to think about what she would do. When he returned, she informed him that after prayer, she had decided to stay with him and stand beside him as he walked out his journey of repentance.

The conversations had continued with his children, their extended family, and the Bethel leadership and staff. Ben described how he had confessed to Bill Johnson and owned up to all the ways he had betrayed his relationships and responsibilities in the Bethel family. Bill had simply responded, "Yes, you did."

"Will you forgive me?" Ben had asked.

And Bill had said, "Yes, I will."

Then Ben had addressed the entire ministry school. With Heather beside him on the platform, Ben explained to the students that he was choosing to remain on staff as an administrative assistant, but would be stepping down from his pastoral role until his mess was cleaned up, which didn't just mean apologizing and asking for forgiveness, but doing the work to repair the heart issues that had led to the sin and rebuilding his life, marriage, and family on a brand-new, stronger, and healthier foundation of trust and connection than existed before he destroyed them. He gave an open invitation for any person affected by his betrayal to reach out to him if they needed so he could clean up the mess with them personally.

For an entire year, Ben's life was fully focused on walking out this repentance. Personal, marriage, and family counseling became a weekly part of life for him, Heather, and their kids. As a couple, Ben and Heather slogged through the process of uncovering and addressing the issues that had been contributing to chronic disconnection in their marriage from the beginning. There was much more to confess, forgive, and unravel than either of them had known, yet even when it was excruciating, they courageously moved toward one another and continued learning how to build a level of emotional honesty, trust, and connection they had never had before. They also worked hard to bring their kids into this new relational culture.

During that season, Ben and Heather navigated interacting with Ben's former intern, who had moved out of their home immediately after bringing the affair to light, but remained in the church community. She and the family both had to decide how to walk out forgiveness and new relational boundaries.

As he had promised, Ben talked with every single person who reached out by phone, email, or in person to talk with him, which by the end of that year numbered well over a hundred. He also sat faithfully at his desk at school every day grading homework, allowing those he used to lead from the platform to see him serving them in the role he had chosen while he cleaned up his mess. The message was clear—he wasn't running away from the mess, and he wasn't acting like things were cleaned up before they were.

At the end of that year, Ben and Heather agreed to update the ministry school students on the progress of their journey of healing. Their children joined them on the platform. Ben described the steps he had taken to build a new lifestyle of living in the light, and the incredible freedom and healing he was experiencing as a result. Heather shared about her own process of forgiveness and the adjustments she had chosen to make to build a new and better connection with Ben. They gave examples of how their children were becoming powerful in expressing their feelings and needs, and even holding them accountable as a couple for the relational standards they had agreed to honor as a family. Though there was still more ground to cover on their healing journey, they acknowledged that love, hope, and joy were filling their lives and home like never before.

The applause from the students at the end of Ben and Heather's testimony had been deafening. People were shouting, crying, hugging, and punching the air as they celebrated this incredible victory. In the months that followed, many of them sought out Ben and Heather and other Bethel staff to let them know how it had impacted them to watch a leader walk out a journey of repentance and reconciliation like this. Most of them said they had never experienced anything like it.

And of course, that ending wasn't really an ending, but the beginning of Ben and Heather not only learning to walk in a lifestyle of freedom, emotional honesty, accountability, and connection, but gaining the authority to equip others to do the same. When Ben eventually returned to a pastoral role in the school—a decision he made in full accord with the church leadership—he was a very different leader. He brought a culture of living in the light to his students, modeling healthy vulnerability by sharing his story, teaching them how to be open with trusted friends and leaders about where they are struggling, and showing them what it means to be a safe place for others to do the same with them.

PUNISHED VS. DISCIPLINED

Most of the leaders in the conference room seemed to be riveted on the edge of their seats as Ben and Heather shared their remarkable journey. By the smiles and hopeful looks I saw around the room, I knew many of them were inspired and encouraged by this redemptive conclusion. But I also knew that wheels were cranking in minds around the room, hungry to understand more about this repentance process and how to replicate it in their environments.

"Does anyone have any questions for Ben and Heather?" I asked.

Li raised his hand first. "How was the decision made for you to step out of ministry, Ben, and for how long? Was that something that Danny or someone else suggested, or were you told that you were being removed from your position?"

"No one told me, 'This is what is going to happen. You're going to do this, this, and this,'" Ben answered. "As I talked with Dann and Danny, the question we were all asking ourselves was, 'What is going to make us feel like geniuses here?' Dann and Danny were looking out for the Bethel community and ministry school. They wanted to send the message to our students that they were going to be protected through this process.

My job as a revival pastor involved a lot of one-on-one meetings with students, and we all agreed that most of the students probably wouldn't feel safe to be doing that while I was cleaning up my mess. As for me, my primary concern was saving my marriage. I told them, 'I don't think you can bring me back on staff if my wife isn't beside me.' Only when my marriage is healthy will I feel like a genius for going back to pastor students. So that was the plan we came up with, and I trusted the leadership to tell me when the time was right to return."

Bruce spoke up next. "Ben, what was the biggest difference for you in how you handled this affair versus the first one?"

"The way I describe it is that when the first affair happened, I was punished," Ben said. "I was ashamed, humiliated, and disempowered. The thing I loved and was good at—pastoring people—was taken away from me. The second time, I was disciplined. And here's what I discovered. *Punishment is way easier than discipline.* We think punishment is hard, and it is, but it's nowhere near as hard as actually walking out the process of getting your life cleaned up. My life was a wreck. I liken discipline to open-heart surgery. It's a big operation with a long recovery period. I had to learn a whole new way to live, a whole new way to be me, and I had to be okay with that process taking as long as it took. But in that process, the things that were never addressed the first time—the shame, guilt, and fear—finally got healed. Punishment only made those things grow in my life."

"Did anyone in the church or school choose not to forgive you or trust you again?" Alexandra piped up. "How did you deal with that?"

"There were plenty of people who needed time before they chose to trust me again," Ben nodded. "Many of the students I met with, mostly women, have come back to me, some a year and a half later, and said, 'I waited to see if you were really going to walk this out and if it was real. Thank you for doing what you chose to do. Thank you for staying. Thank you for cleaning up your mess. Thank you for putting the structures in your life that you have now. And I just want to tell you, I forgive you.' Currently, I don't know of anyone who's still angry with me."

Seeing that it was time to wrap up the session, I took the microphone back from Ben and said, "As we close, I want you to go back to what you wrote down about what you would have done in this situation. After hearing how Ben and Heather walked out this journey of repentance, reconciliation, and restoration, what would you do differently?"

The leaders once again bent over their papers. After a long pause, I saw Walter's hand go up in the back. "I have a question for you, Danny. *What would you have done if Ben hadn't repented?*"

CHAPTER 2

THE PUNISHMENT PARADIGM

Whenever I share stories of repentance, reconciliation, and restoration like Ben and Heather's, people have two basic responses.

First, people celebrate these stories. They're the kind of relational victories we all hope for. There's nothing more heartbreaking than betrayal, and nothing more beautiful and powerful than people coming through that experience with repaired, redeemed, and resurrected connections. Believers know that this is a miracle of grace. It's the gospel of Jesus at work.

Second, people view these stories as outliers. More often, we encounter stories of people who don't repent, broken relationships that stay broken, and the resulting debris field of people living in unresolved pain. And so, after celebrating the success stories with me, most people want me to address what feels like a much more pressing question: "What do you do when the person doesn't repent?"

The short answer to that question is that until someone who has violated or betrayed a relationship repents, there can be no reconciliation or restoration. In such cases, you are dealing with a person who is refusing to clean up their mess or change, which means they will violate and betray again. They are insisting on remaining as a selfish predator in their relationships. Most often, our main priorities in dealing with them are going to be managing ourselves well and, depending on our position of authority in their lives, introducing appropriate consequences that will prevent or limit them from causing more damage. I have walked with people through processes that resulted in job terminations and divorces because they refused to change. If Ben hadn't repented, both those results would have been likely in his situation. I should clarify that in cases where someone is breaking the laws of the land, they pass beyond the jurisdiction of the church and home and must be handed them over to government authorities. In those cases, the city, state, or federal judgment will be enforcing certain consequences for their crimes. A child molester is going to jail a hundred percent of the time, whether or not they repent. There have been situations, both during my first career in social work and later as a pastor, in which I have called on law enforcement and child protective services to deal with people who refused to stop acting in violent ways toward their family members. In cases where there was repentance, I continued to walk with people through that process, but I was not determining or administrating the legal consequences for their behavior.

I will have more to say about what to do when people don't repent later in this book. But first, we need take a few steps back. Everyone is anxious to learn how to deal with an unrepentant person without really understanding how we arrive at putting that label on someone or why so many of our betrayal stories unfold the way they do.

One of the powerful things about Ben's story is that it puts on display two very different ways of responding to a betrayal. He had two affairs. Both times he was a pastor, and the church leadership took the role of leading him through a process of dealing with his sin. But while both processes ultimately resulted in him returning to church leadership and keeping his family intact, only the second process involved genuine repentance. In the first process, Ben's leaders and community—and perhaps even Ben himself—probably would have labeled him "repentant." But we know that whatever he did, it wasn't repentance. Why? Because twelve years later, he did it again. Genuine repentance can always be identified by its fruit, and its fruit is enduring change—transformation. At the very least (and it is, as we shall see, much more), the transformation produced by genuine repentance looks like the person not continuing to violate their relationships in the same way.

Why did Ben not repent the first time? Was it because he had a hard, "unrepentant" heart? Not at all. He gave a heartfelt confession and apology to his congregation and asked his wife for forgiveness. He felt terrible about his sin and had no intention of cheating a second time. He worked hard for twelve years not to fall into that hole again. The real reason he didn't actually repent was twofold: 1) he didn't know how to repent, and 2) no one in his environment required repentance or guided him through it.

But there is an even deeper reason behind this reason. In the first process Ben went through to deal with his sin, repentance was not the goal or priority. In fact, in some very real ways, his experience actually discouraged him from truly repenting.

BEFORE AND AFTER PUNISHMENT

"I'm afraid to be seen and known, because I'm afraid that if I do anything wrong, I'm going to be punished."

When Ben identified this as the problem at the root of his lifestyle of isolation and disconnection, which had led to him illegitimately seeking comfort and connection with his intern, it didn't take long for him to see the irony of his situation. In his words, what he had experienced in the wake of his first affair was "punishment." Yet the fear of reliving that experience had ultimately led him right back into the same behavior that had caused it in the first place.

How did this happen?

Let's consider the nature of Ben's punishment. The word "punishment" often evokes harsh and painful consequences like spanking, fines, prison, excommunication, or the death penalty. Arguably, the consequences imposed on Ben by his church leadership and other relationships fell on the mild end of the punishment spectrum. He wasn't removed from the community or church staff. He was allowed to return to his former position after a season. His wife didn't divorce him.

We also expect that "offenders" are likely to be resistant to punishment to some degree. But Ben was a willing participant in his punishment process. He ceased all bad behavior and demonstrated only good behavior. He confessed before the congregation. He served faithfully in his post as the church janitor. He stayed with Heather and did all he could to be a good husband to her. Again, as far as anyone knew, he had "repented" as best he could.

Yet from the moment his sin came to light, Ben was branded with an invisible scarlet letter of shame. In every step of the punishment process—confessing, apologizing, and stepping out of ministry for a time—he owned this shame more deeply. He had broken one of the ten commandments. He was an adulterer, a failed husband. He was also a failed Christian leader. As a church kid who had grown up to be a pastor, he had spent his whole life in a culture where the expectation of godly leaders was that they weren't supposed to have any problems with sin.

On top of this, Ben was left in pain of his shame and sin with no real way to find healing. None of the steps Ben took helped him identify the problem at the root of his infidelity or empowered him and Heather to repair the disconnection in their marriage. Neither did Ben find the tools and support to build a healthy lifestyle of walking in the light with trusted friends and colleagues and become a more authentic, transparent leader, husband, father, and man. Though Heather forgave him, the best they could do was bandage over the broken areas and try to limp forward. The same was true in his other relationships and in his pastoral role.

Ben's experience of punishment was being caught in a place where he was shamed by his mess, couldn't clean it up, and then had to try to live up to the expectation that he would never mess up again. What could Ben do but conclude, *I never want to go through that pain again. I guess the only way to avoid it is to try harder to behave well*?

On the other side of punishment, Ben simply redoubled his efforts to live out his old belief that he wasn't allowed to have problems, which ended up meaning that he learned to *hide better.* When other leaders asked him how he was doing, he had the right answer ready to give: "I'm awesome. I'm great." He did the same in his marriage, playing the strong husband who was always there to take care of his wife and had no needs or struggles of his own. He also continued to hide from God and himself, which is how in over twelve years of intense behavior management, Ben never really took a good look at the beliefs and motives that were driving him. He didn't see that the same issues that had led to his first affair—shame, isolation, disconnection from his own heart, and the fear of punishment—were the same issues behind his "perfect" performance record as a pastor and husband.

Ben also couldn't see that his fear of punishment and his strategy of hiding through good behavior were themselves connected to a fundamental goal that, by its nature, positioned him to eventually betray and violate his relationships—the goal of self-preservation. When our goal is self-preservation, the fear of punishment only adds fuel to the fire of our self-interested behavior. We may succeed in stopping certain bad behaviors and demonstrating good behavior, but it will still be good behavior with selfish motives, which is incapable of producing anything truly good in the long run. We will either break down and sin again, as Ben eventually did, or we will become the worst kind of "good" people—self-righteous, hypocritical Pharisees.

In summary, Ben's experience of punishment only reinforced everything that was already going on inside him when he sinned the first time:

	Before Punishment	**After Punishment**
Core Belief	Christian leaders aren't allowed to have problems.	Christian leaders aren't allowed to have problems.
Motive	Fear of punishment, shame	Fear of punishment, shame
Behavior Strategy	Hide through good behavior	Hide through good behavior
Goal	Self-preservation	Self-preservation

This is how Ben's fear of punishment led him right back into doing the thing that had gotten him punished in the first place. Nothing in Ben's experience of punishment showed him a path to repentance. Repentance is all about radically changing the core beliefs, motives, and goal of our heart, which is the only thing that produces genuine, lasting transformation in our behavior. Instead of inviting Ben to pursue this kind of change, punishment *actively discouraged* him from changing by amplifying what was already going on in his heart.

A CULTURE OF PUNISHMENT

Ben's experience of and response to punishment is far from isolated. It is all too common and recognizable—it is, in fact, what we expect. Our default assumption is that offenders will re-offend, even if they try hard not to. That's what usually happens in our world. This assumption is part of the belief system that drives our classic reactions to offense when we encounter it.

Consider the reactions of the audience members I introduced in Chapter 1. We saw:

- A wrathful desire to avenge the victims by punishing the offender. (Chuck)
- The belief that Christian leaders shouldn't have problems, especially at a "good" church. (Alexandra)
- Shame, righteous indignation, and condemnation of sin. (Li)
- The need to discipline the offender to discourage future offense. (Walter)
- Fear of punishment. (Carolyn and Bruce)

Imagine if someone had told the pre-repentance part of Ben's story in a social media post or article. These kinds of reactions would *dominate* the comments section! In fact, one of the primary things social media has done is create the opportunity for humans to verbally unleash their reactions to sin and offense without limits. This has only put on undeniable display the fact that our reactions typically have something to do with punishment—the desire for punishment, a call for punishment, a conviction that punishment is appropriate, or a fear of being punished ourselves.

These reactions are understandable. They are also deeply problematic—for the same reason that Ben's punishment experience was problematic. The reason we turn first to thoughts of punishment instead of repentance is that in our heart of hearts, we believe the same things Ben believed about offense and punishment. We are motivated by the same fear of punishment and shame. We are attempting to hide and remain small targets, especially through good behavior. And we are operating with the same goal of self-preservation. On the inside, to varying degrees, we are just like him. We are operating from a belief system I call the *punishment paradigm*.

For most of us, the punishment paradigm was formed in us when we were tiny. When we broke the rules, made a mess, or did something our parents disapproved of, we were "disciplined." Our parents inflicted some form of pain on us to send the message that our behavior was bad and unacceptable. We were spanked, yelled at, or deprived of something we wanted. Our power and freedom were taken away. We were scared, intimidated, and controlled. And we reacted in one of two ways. If we were "strong-willed," we rebelled against the punishment and continued to behave badly. If we were "compliant" or "obedient," we "learned our lesson" and changed our behavior. But both responses were driven by the same motive: fear of punishment. In truth, we all learned the same lesson. We didn't learn to reject bad behavior because it violates ourselves, people, and relationships, or to love good behavior for its own sake. We learned to fear punishment.

We also learned shame. "Shame is the fear of disconnection," defines Brené Brown. "It's the fear that something we've done or failed to do, an ideal that we've not lived up to, or a goal that we've not accomplished makes us unworthy of connection . . . *Shame is the intensely painful feeling or experience of believing that we are flawed and therefore unworthy of love and belonging.*"[2] For many of us growing up, our misbehavior, flaws, and failures got linked to disconnection—the relational pain of rejection, disapproval, scorn, and criticism—through our experiences with punishment. This opened the door for a core belief in our unworthiness to settle in our hearts, which in turn began to define an identity and narrative driven by the fear of disconnection.

For some, the shame narrative sounded like this: "To avoid the pain of disconnection, I must not expose my flaws or failures. I will hide—especially through (as Brown puts it) 'pleasing, performing, and

---

[2] Brené Brown, *Daring Greatly* (New York, NY: Avery, 2012), Kindle Edition, 78.

perfecting.'" Those of us who bought into this narrative often embraced identities like "the shy kid," "the over-achiever," or "the good girl/boy."

For others, the narrative was, "There's no way I can hide my messiness—I'm not even going to try. I'm going to protect myself from the pain of disconnection by creating a world where I either numb out with pleasure, or where I make the rules and get people to fear me instead of the other way around." Those of us who ran with this as a life-script often ended up taking on identities like "the wild child" or "the rebel."

Again, we see two behavior strategies. One is to keep the rules, be "good," and try to fit in with the crowd. The other is to defy or redefine the rules and refuse to fit in. However, both ultimately point to the same goal: self-preservation. They are both attempts to control and manipulate our interactions with other people to save ourselves from punishment.

Guess what ends up being one of the things we use to pursue this goal? Punishment. When other people scare us, offend us, or hurt us, we turn around and use the same tools on them that were used on us. If they are our child, we scold, spank, ground, or remove privileges to curb the bad behavior. If they are our spouse or a friend, we attack with criticism or freeze them out with distance. If they are someone who disagrees with us on social media, we one-up them with a vicious rebuttal. If they are a leader or public figure who fails to live up to our expectations and makes us feel insecure or powerless, we unleash our condemnation and call for his or her removal. If we are a leader who feels threatened by an opponent, we build a strategy to take them down. The stronger the fear of punishment and the voice of shame are in our hearts, the more we use the threat of punishment and disconnection to protect ourselves. The harshest punishment comes from those of us who are most driven by fear and shame.

Beneath these reactions is a deep and haunting conviction. Shame tells us that we are unworthy of connection. The corollary is this: we deserve disconnection. We deserve punishment. This is the belief that fuels human *wrath*. It's what produces righteous indignation and vengeance toward the offenses of others, and self-criticism and every form of self-destruction in the face of our own. It also fuels hopelessness that people—ourselves included—can change. Behind our efforts to intimidate people into compliance and good behavior, and our striving to create the perception of perfection in ourselves, we are running from a voice telling us we cannot overcome the flaws that make us worthy of punishment, and that eventually, that punishment will catch up to us.

The Punishment Paradigm	
Core Belief	My flaws and failures make me unworthy of love, belonging, and connection. I deserve disconnection and punishment. So does everyone else with flaws and failures.
Motive	Fear of punishment/disconnection
Behavior Strategies	1. Avoid punishment—either by hiding and fitting in through 'pleasing, perfecting, and performing,' or by refusing to fit in by rebelling and making my own rules. 2. Punish others when they scare, hurt, or offend me.
Goal	Self-preservation

Sooner or later, as it did for Ben, our fear leads us right into the experience we are trying so desperately to avoid. Life in the punishment paradigm is a catch-22, an endless cycle of fear, control, failure, and punishment where we end up saying, like Job, "For the thing I greatly feared has come upon me" (Job 3:25 NKJV).

Yet the real tragedy is not that we stumble, fall, make a mess, and are punished. It's that we continue to remain enslaved to the punishment paradigm because we don't encounter the invitation to be delivered from our fear of punishment, shame, and the whole hopeless project of self-preservation in the one place that exists to offer that invitation—the body of Christ.

CONFRONTING OUR ADDICTION

When I joined the senior leadership team at Bethel Church, it didn't take long for situations requiring "church discipline" to find their way to my office. My training and experience in social work and foster care, along with pastoral ministry, had equipped me with certain tools, skills, and wisdom for confronting people who were making messes in our environment. However, there were aspects of my approach that made some of the other senior leaders a little nervous. Here were the basic guidelines of this approach:

1. The primary goal of the confrontation is to invite people to take the path of repentance, reconciliation, and restoration of trust and connection.
2. If the person refuses to take this path, we keep our love on and communicate that the option to repent was still open, but until the person chooses that option, there can be no reconciliation or restoration. We will therefore introduce appropriate consequences to show them that they have effectively removed themselves from trust and connection.
3. If they do repent, then we will respond with forgiveness, reconciliation, and restoration of trust and connection.

The thing that made the other leaders nervous was what was missing in #3: punishment. There were no prescribed "steps" the repentant person had to take to clean up their mess—no mandated public confession, no minimum leave of absence for them to be "disciplined." Sure, they all agreed *in theory* with the sermon I began to preach everywhere—"Unpunishable"—where I laid out the theological and practical support for my approach. But as I began to implement it, they asked me, "Are you sure this is going to work?"

I assured them that it would. Yes, I knew this approach wasn't the norm in most churches. I didn't yet have an overwhelming list of examples of restored church leaders I could bring out to convince everyone. But I knew it would work for two reasons. First, I believed it lined up with the truth of the gospel and the way it transforms people. Second, as a social worker who had trained parents, and as a parent and foster parent myself, I had seen how effective (and radically transformative for both parents and children) it was to remove punishment as a tool for disciplining children and replace it with tools that allowed children to learn from the consequences of their choices while encouraging them to pursue the goal of *connection*. Conversely, I had seen how unhelpful punishment was as a tool for disciplining children. Over and over, here's what I saw to be true about punishment:

- It positions you as opponents, rather than partners, in the discipline process.
- It does not empower people to clean up their mess.
- It produces shame and disconnection.
- It distracts people from learning about the real consequences of their choices. Instead, they only learn the fear of punishment.

Situation by situation, I applied my approach. Sadly, but not unsurprisingly, there were people who chose not to take the path of repentance, reconciliation, and restoration when it was offered to them. But wonderfully, there were many who did. Josh and Robin Biddlecomb, whose story I tell in Chapter 1 of my book *Culture of Honor*, were one standout example. They were an engaged couple, both students in the Bethel School of Supernatural Ministry, who got pregnant outside of marriage and walked out an incredible, miraculous journey of repentance, reconciliation, and restoration with each other and the school. Ben, of course, was another. Over time, as I traveled and preached the "Unpunishable" message and was invited to consult with church leaders around the globe in various disciplinary cases, I was privileged to witness many more people take this path. And every single one proved the same thing—that those who choose the path of repentance, reconciliation, and restoration *do not need to be punished.* This path, in fact, is the path where they finally are set free from the toxic punishment paradigm and empowered to pursue an entirely new belief system, identity, narrative, motivation, strategy, and goal.

But getting set free from the punishment paradigm is not easy. When 1 John 4:18 says that perfect loves "casts out" fear, which has to do with punishment, it is using deliverance language for a reason. We are dealing with the absolute heart of spiritual warfare when we invite people to let God rewrite the paradigm they have lived from their whole lives. As I have waded into this battle with people who are bravely choosing to walk this journey of transformation, it has exposed just how deeply the punishment paradigm has a hold in the hearts of believers.

One of the things I have seen repeatedly is that even when someone repents, Christians still want the person to be punished. When Heather decided to stay with Ben and fight for their marriage after his second affair, she was somewhat surprised that it was her Christian friends who struggled most with this decision and urged her to divorce him. Her non-Christian friends more readily accepted and supported her choice to forgive and reconcile with him. Likewise, when I have assured church leadership teams that one of their fallen leaders has chosen repentance and is on the road to restoration, there is usually someone who insists that certain punitive steps still be taken—not for the purpose of restoring the leader, but to calm the fears of the congregation and assure them that the leader is being disciplined.

The challenge with confronting the punishment paradigm, as with any lie we believe, is that it feels right to us. Even though the reality of punishment has brought the torment of fear, isolation, striving, shame, and every other toxic thing into our hearts and lives, we can't imagine life without it. We have a love affair with punishment. We are addicted to it. Even though we're afraid of it, even though we know it doesn't work, even though it makes us miserable—we can't give it up. Why?

First, we're addicted to the false sense of power, control, and safety punishment gives us. When we feel scared, powerless, and full of righteous anger toward someone, punishment is the familiar tool we grab to protect ourselves and try to get our power back.

Second, punishment really requires nothing from us except to act like a victim of pain. As Ben said, "Punishment is easy." We don't have to grieve the pain we caused others, humble ourselves, and ask for forgiveness. We don't have to bravely confront the broken places in us that led to making a mess. We don't have to vulnerably show our broken heart to someone who hurt us and forgive them. We don't have to take on the responsibility to clean up our mess, or the sacrificial love to walk alongside someone as they clean up their mess. We don't have to learn, grow, or transform. Ultimately, we don't have to make the difficult transition to leave the goal of self-preservation behind and do the courageous work of pursuing the goal of connection.

For those of us who have lived all our lives in a punishment paradigm, there's a third reason we don't want to give it up—we don't know there's any other option. We may have heard people talk about a better way to deal with offenses—a way that doesn't minimize or cover them up, doesn't retaliate in anger, doesn't hold on to bitterness, and actually leads to the pain being healed and wrong being made right. But many of us have never really seen or experienced it for ourselves. We just haven't seen how the punishment-free process for cleaning up our messes really works.

In the chapters ahead, my goal is to lay out a pathway to freedom from the punishment paradigm and life in the punishment-free relationships with God, ourselves, and one another we were created for. We'll start with the biblical story that tells us the spiritual roots of the punishment paradigm and why we love it so much, and how the gospel sets us free to live in the paradigm of new covenant love and family. Then we'll get practical about how we walk out the journey of repentance, reconciliation, and restoration in our own lives, and how we can build an "unpunishable" culture in our homes, businesses, churches, and communities where everyone is invited, encouraged, and supported to take this journey as well. It's time for the body of Christ to end our love affair with punishment and learn to walk in perfect love.

CHAPTER 3

WHY DO WE LOVE PUNISHMENT SO MUCH?

The Bible shows us that the punishment paradigm isn't some socially constructed, cultural phenomenon. It is a universal human experience with deep spiritual roots. In fact, this paradigm came to be at the very beginning, when humankind fell from God through sin. Let's look back at the story in Genesis 3:

> Now the serpent was more crafty than any of the wild animals the LORD God had made. He said to the woman, "Did God really say, 'You must not eat from any tree in the garden'?" The woman said to the serpent, "We may eat fruit from the trees in the garden, but God did say, 'You must not eat fruit from the tree that is in the middle of the garden, and you must not touch it, or you will die.'" "You will not certainly die," the serpent said to the woman. "For God knows that when you eat from it your eyes will be opened, and you will be like God, knowing good and evil." When the woman saw that the fruit of the tree was good for food and pleasing to the eye, and also desirable for

> gaining wisdom, she took some and ate it. She also gave some to her husband, who was with her, and he ate it. (Genesis 3:1-6)

Eating the fruit of the tree of the knowledge of good and evil wasn't about eating a fruit—it was about human beings trying to define good and evil, right and wrong, for themselves. Sin always involves us trying to make the rules. Wanting to make the rules means wanting to rule ourselves—to be our own gods. It is *idolatry*, which the Bible equates with spiritual *adultery*—betraying our relationship with God and putting someone else—ourselves—in His place.

How did Adam and Eve end up switching teams and attempting to make the rules? It began with a deception. The enemy planted lies in their minds about God. They bought into his story and believed God was holding out on them, that He wasn't good, that they couldn't trust His rules or His reign in their lives. Tim Keller writes:

> Sin always begins with the character assassination of God. We believe that God has put us in a world of delights but has determined that he will not give them to us if we obey him. This is the lie of the serpent, the original temptation of Satan to Adam and Eve that brought about the Fall (Genesis 3:4–5). The serpent told the human race that disobeying God was the only way to realize their fullest happiness and potential, and this delusion has sunk deep into every human heart . . . This is really the most fundamental temptation that there has ever been in the world, and the original sin. Specific details may vary, but the deep heart song of "I have to look out for myself" is always there.[3]

[3] Keller, Timothy. *The Prodigal Prophet* (New York, NY: Penguin Publishing Group, 2018) Kindle Edition, pp. 137-139.

"I have to look out for myself"—this is the motto of self-preservation. As the consequences of Adam and Eve's sin play out in Genesis 3, we see self-preservation, along with the other elements of the punishment paradigm, come into play.

NAKED AND AFRAID

The first consequence Adam and Eve experience is the shameful awareness of their nakedness: "Then the eyes of both of them were opened, and they realized they were naked; so they sewed fig leaves together and made coverings for themselves" (Genesis 3:7). This verse contrasts with the last verse of Genesis 2: "Adam and his wife were both naked, and they felt no shame" (Genesis 2:25).

There's an interesting Hebrew word play going on here. The word translated "naked" comes from the same word used to describe the serpent, "crafty" (Genesis 3:1), and means "to be or make bare."[4] The crafty serpent convinced Adam and Eve that they were going to "lay bare" the forbidden wisdom God was supposedly keeping from them and become like Him. Instead, they laid bare themselves and became like the serpent, not like God.

The Hebrew word for "shame" means "disappointed" and "disconcerted."[5] Adam and Eve were disappointed when what they'd hoped would happen by eating the fruit didn't happen. Yes, "their eyes were opened," just as the serpent had promised. But instead of seeing whatever "God-likeness" they had expected to see, they saw nakedness. This was *disconcerting*—the word means "to throw into confusion."

---

[4] H6191 - `aram - Strong's Hebrew Lexicon (KJV). Retrieved from https://www.blueletterbible.org//lang/lexicon/lexicon.cfm?Strongs=H6191&t=KJV

[5] "H954 - buwsh – Strong's Hebrew Lexicon (NIV)." Blue Letter Bible. Accessed 24 July, 2019. https://www.blueletterbible.org//lang/lexicon/lexicon.cfm?Strongs=H954&t=NIV

Have you ever tried something that you were totally confident would work, and it didn't? You thought you had a foolproof plan of action, but the results were the complete opposite of what you'd expected? I certainly have—on multiple occasions. And I can tell you that there is nothing more disappointing and disconcerting than the experience of failure. It makes us feel *exposed*.

For example, over twenty years ago I experienced one of the most excruciating failures of my life. It was a situation where I was absolutely convinced that I was doing the right thing . . . until someone showed me in a moment that it was absolutely the wrong thing. Like many big mistakes, this was not the work of a moment, but a situation that unfolded over several years, beginning in 1995, when I replaced Bill Johnson as the senior pastor of a small Assemblies of God church in the mountains of Northern California. Upon stepping into the role, I received a provisional pastoring credential in good faith that I would complete two years of course study to officially become a credentialed pastor with the Assemblies of God, and several more years of service to be fully ordained. Having just completed eight years of university study and an internship to finish my bachelor's and master's in social work, however, the prospect of more academic training was unappealing and something I didn't believe I needed. So, I put the studies on the back burner and turned all my attention to building the leadership team, nurturing the health of the church, and expanding the buildings on the church property.

I had all but forgotten about the credentialing requirements when, out of the blue, I received a letter from the Assemblies district office saying, in effect, "It's been almost five years and we have not heard from you about this task we assigned you. Remember the credential you need to hold the position you have?"

When I read the letter, a chill ran down my spine. To me, the idea of going back to book study sounded like eating cantaloupe every day for the next two years. I was already succeeding as a pastor without it. The church was thriving, numbers were up, our building was less than a year away from completion. Complying with this burdensome formality was not anywhere close to a priority for me.

So, I came up with an idea. I went to the elders and proposed that we drop out of the denomination. They quickly agreed with me that our ties to the district office were weak and consisted primarily of paying membership dues, which didn't seem to be essential to the success of the church. Thrilled with their support for my plan, which would neatly eliminate my credentialing dilemma, I decided to run it by Bill Johnson before sending off an official letter to the district office terminating our association with the Assemblies of God.

A few weeks later, Bill met with our leadership team for an update on how things were going. After regaling him with all the good news about what God was doing at the church, I sensed the moment was right to bring up the credentialing problem and the solution I had devised.

Bill nodded his head as I talked, which seemed to suggest that he understood and approved of the course of action I was laying out. After I finished, he cleared his throat and said, "So what you're saying is . . ." followed by a summary of my explanation. When I had confirmed that he had understood me, he continued to nod while he said, "You can do what you are suggesting if you are certain that you want to dishonor thirty-plus years of the lives that have poured into what you now call 'your ministry' at this church. You've inherited a great deal that you did nothing to earn. If you would like to dishonor that legacy, then go ahead and sever your ties. And, if you would like to sow rebellion and division into your leadership culture, then this is how you do it. Go ahead."

I felt like I'd been kicked in the chest by a mule. My head was buzzing. The elder team was dead silent. Everyone in the room knew that Bill's assessment of my plan was absolutely right. I was standing alone, completely exposed, in the middle of the mess I'd created. I didn't know it was a mess until that moment—no one had pushed back on my scheme up to that point, so I had been blinded by confidence that I was right. But with just a few sentences, Bill's rebuke had showed me what a terrible mess it was. Talk about *disconcerting.*

Waves of hot shame surged through me. My face and ears felt like they were on fire. I had disappointed Bill Johnson. If there was anyone besides Jesus and my wife that I didn't want to disappoint, it was Bill. Disappointing him meant I had disappointed myself in being the leader and man I wanted to be. I was crushed.

When my ability to breathe returned, I stuttered, "What do I do, Bill? The Assemblies is going to revoke my credentials and replace me as pastor here."

"You know what to do," Bill said simply.

"I do?"

"Repent."

Thankfully, I did just that. I humbled myself and apologized to Bill and to his father, Earl, who had secured the provisional credential for me in the first place. Earl went before the district assembly and ask them to have mercy on me for failing to complete the courses. They agreed to extend my grace period, and I went to work on the requirements. In the end, my studies were interrupted when Bill invited me to come on staff at Bethel Church in Redding, California, where I didn't need the credential to pastor. What I did have, however, was an unforgettable experience of failure, shame, and disappointment, which, through repentance, was redeemed into learning and growth.

Adam and Eve, on the other hand, didn't repent on the other side of their mess. They remained in that painful state of nakedness and exposure—not only of their physical bodies, but of their souls. The failure of sin has a way of shattering our confidence and trust in what we know of ourselves and the world. It makes us feel like something is wrong with us. The shattering of trust is an experience of *disconnection*. In Adam and Eve's case, sin introduced disconnection with God, themselves, each other, and creation. This psychological and spiritual trauma left them feeling unprotected, powerless, and threatened, which in turn produced shame—the fear of disconnection.

HIDING AND BLAME-SHIFTING

How did Adam and Eve react to this fear? They hid. Instead of running to God to cover and protect them—and ultimately, to restore their shattered trust and connection—they made coverings for themselves. They both agreed that self-protection was the way to go, and continued with this strategy when God showed up looking for them:

> Then the man and his wife heard the sound of the LORD God as he was walking in the garden in the cool of the day, and they hid from the LORD God among the trees of the garden. But the LORD God called to the man, "Where are you?" He answered, "I heard you in the garden, and I was afraid because I was naked; so I hid." (Genesis 3:8-10)

It's important to see that Adam and Eve's fear of God was a consequence of *sin*. God did nothing to shame, scare, or punish them in any way. He was not the one who told them they were naked. The only thing God had done—besides creating them in joy, surrounding them with beauty, and empowering them to rule and reign the planet with Him—was to give them a command and a very clear reason for it: "You must not eat from the tree of the knowledge of good and evil, for when you eat from it you will certainly die" (Genesis 2:17). And that's exactly what was happening when they made coverings and hid from God. No, Adam and Eve didn't "return to dust" the moment they ate the fruit. But spiritually, they became disconnected from the source of life, God Himself. The moment "their eyes were opened," they fell into spiritual darkness and couldn't see their way back to the light. Buying into the enemy's assassination of God's character rendered them unable to recover a true vision of who He was—they became locked in their false view of the universe and its Creator, and it was this view that produced the fear of punishment in their hearts.

Adam and Eve's bondage to their deception was "death" because it prevented them from finding their way back to God. It trapped them in a spiritual nightmare, a darkened, distorted reality in which resubmitting to God's authority and repairing their connection—repentance and reconciliation—appeared scary, impossible, and even undesirable. This was the catch-22 into which the enemy had drawn them—to step out from the covering of God's authority, attempt to make their own rules, see this backfire spectacularly, and then find that their hearts were bound, through shame and fear, to the addiction of continuing to try to make the rules apart from God, even though doing so would only produce more disconnection, shame, and fear.

We see this bondage play out in Adam and Eve's responses to God asking them if they had eaten the fruit:

> And he said, "Who told you that you were naked? Have you eaten from the tree that I commanded you not to eat from?" The man said, "The woman you put here with me—she gave me some fruit from the tree, and I ate it." Then the LORD God said to the woman, "What is this you have done?" The woman said, "The serpent deceived me, and I ate." (Genesis 3:11-13)

Up to this point, Adam and Eve have colluded in making and trying to manage this mess—eating the fruit, making coverings from fig leaves, and hiding. But when God asks questions to hold them accountable, they go fully into "every man for himself" mode, doubling down on their new goal of self-preservation by blame-shifting and throwing each other under the bus. Adam not only doesn't repent, he blames Eve and God as though they were ganging up on him. He is the first "victim" in human history. He presents himself as powerless over what he decided to do, shifting responsibility away from himself and accusing the only other two people on the planet for his situation. This only serves to widen the wedges of disconnection they've created between themselves, God, and one another. This is the self-sabotaging dynamic of shame. After disconnecting from God through sin and experiencing the pain of shame, Adam and Eve's fear of disconnection leads them to react in ways that further betray and violate connection.

We see this same cycle play out in our lives whenever we decide to be powerless victims, even in the most seemingly innocuous situations. A common example I use is of a couple being awakened in the middle of the night by the cries of their baby. Neither one moves as they wait to see who will volunteer first to tend to the child. The husband hears the voice of his heart nudging him, *Get up. Take care of the baby and let your wife sleep. She's tired.* But he doesn't listen to that voice, and the instant he chooses the interests of self over connection, another internal voice speaks up—the voice of blame and self-justification. *Look at her—she's not getting up either. What kind of a mother would lie there and let her baby cry? A bad mother. A lazy mother. What kind of a wife would let her husband, who works so hard to provide for his family, be robbed of sleep? A bad wife. A selfish wife.*

Before he knows it, this man is seriously entertaining slanderous lies about the woman he vowed to love and cherish. Why? Because the moment he betrayed his heart by refusing to listen to its voice, the voice of love, he opened the door to shame and deception. Through the framework of this deception, his wife becomes the bad guy and he the powerless victim who now has every right to keep lying in bed. Disconnecting from his heart leads him to disconnect from his wife and defend his decision through blame and self-justification. Unless he repents and chooses to be powerful by listening to the voice of love, he will continue down the path of destroying his marriage.

ENTER PUNISHMENT

God does three things in response to this conversation with Adam and Eve. First, He issues a series of pronouncements describing the various types of conflict, pain, and struggle they will experience because of their sin. Basically, everything He created and commissioned humans to do—to co-labor in ruling the animals, tending the ground, and being fruitful and multiplying—would now be full of pain and suffering (see Genesis 3:14-19). Then, God replaced the fig-leaf coverings Adam and Eve had made for themselves with ones He made from skins (see Genesis 3:21). Finally, God banished Adam and Eve from the garden to prevent them from eating from the tree of life.

Again, it's important to remember that Adam and Eve had not repented for their sin. They clung to their shame, blaming, and distance from God and one another. Without repentance, there could be no reconciliation or restoration. So, God explained what life would be like for them living in that choice and showed them that He was still there with them, mitigating the consequences to a certain degree. He essentially said, "I created you to function out of connection with Me and one another. Choosing self-protection over reconnection cuts you off from the only thing that causes you to flourish in every department of life, and that means life is going to be *really hard* for you." The intention in God's other two actions shows us His tone in this pronouncement. Clothing Adam and Eve and banishing them from the garden were fatherly acts of provision and protection. He protected them from the disaster of eating from the tree of life and becoming permanently enslaved to the enemy, sin, and death, and He provided them with superior garments for life in the harsher conditions outside the garden. Even as He introduced them to the tough consequences of their sin, He was caring for them. Behind the Father's words, He was showing them, "I'm really sad for you."

Yet we can also imagine how, to a deceived and unrepentant Adam and Eve, these consequences might seem like punishment. And biblically, as we'll see in a moment, they were punishment. In fact, to be left in a state of disconnection with God, others, and ourselves is the worst punishment we can experience as human beings. The problem was that this state was one in which Adam and Eve had put themselves and getting out of it was . . . complicated.

We see a hint of this complication in the next story in Genesis. One question that naturally comes up at this point is, *could* Adam and Eve have repented for sin in the garden? Could they have experienced reconciliation and restoration with God and prevented the human race's long legacy of bondage to sin, shame, and death? Well, in Genesis 4, we see an answer play out in the second generation of Adam and Eve's family. In this story, we see the birth of religion—humanity's attempts to engage with God in their fallen state. Cain and Abel each bring God an offering of results from their work. For whatever reason, God looks favorably on Abel's offering, but not Cain's, and Cain is *not happy* about this. When God confronts Cain about his anger, He says, "Why are you angry? Why is your face downcast? If you do what is right, will you not be accepted? But if you do not do what is right, sin is crouching at your door; it desires to have you, but you must rule over it" (Genesis 4:6-7). God implies that Cain has a choice to change his behavior—to repent—and enter into acceptance and reconnection. If he does this, he will *rule over sin.*

But Cain does not take this opportunity. He gives in to his anger and sins by murdering his brother. When God confronts him the second time, Cain, like his parents did in the garden, attempts to avoid accountability: "I don't know . . . am I my brother's keeper?" (Genesis 4:9). Once again, God responds by announcing the consequences of Cain's sin and lack of repentance—he is fired from his job as a gardener and condemned to be a "restless wanderer on the earth" (Genesis 4:12). God is setting another limit like he did with Cain's parents.

Cain's next words contain the first mention of "punishment" in the Bible:

> Cain said to the LORD, "My punishment is more than I can bear. Today you are driving me from the land, and I will be hidden from your presence; I will be a restless wanderer on the earth, and whoever finds me will kill me." (Genesis 4:13-14)

The Hebrew word translated "punishment" here is *avon*, which is also commonly translated "perversity, depravity, iniquity, guilt." The word includes both the act of sin and its consequences. Bible scholar Tim Mackie explains:

> [*Avon*] refers not only to distorted behavior, but also to the crooked consequences—the hurt people, the broken relationships, the cycles of retaliation. You find this idea in the biblical phrase "to punish," which in biblical Hebrew is "to visit someone's *avon* upon them"—that is, to let them sit in the consequences of their crooked choices . . . This is actually the main way biblical authors talk about God's response to human *avon*—letting people experience the crooked consequences of their choices. This is the meaning of the common biblical phrase "to bear your iniquity," or in Hebrew, to "carry" your *avon*. God

> gives people the dignity of carrying the consequences of their bad decisions.[6]

Look how Cain perceives and interprets his punishment. He says that being kicked off his land will mean that he is hidden from God's presence. That is, he won't just be unable to work as a gardener anymore—he will be condemned to live in shame and disconnection. And in his new life as a "restless wanderer," he will be haunted by the unending sense of impending doom that what he did to his brother will happen to him—"whoever finds me will kill me."

God's response is interesting: "But the LORD said to him, 'Not so; anyone who kills Cain will suffer vengeance seven times over.' Then the LORD put a mark on Cain so that no one who found him would kill him" (Genesis 4:13-15). God does not say "I will avenge anyone who kills you"—He simply creates a way, by marking Cain, of letting people know, "If you do to this man what he did to his brother, it will turn out seven times worse for you." It's a warning about how violence escalates and brings about those cycles of retaliation and retribution. Yet despite this warning, humans continue down the path of sin. Within a few generations, we see one of Cain's great-great-great-grandsons, Lamech, committing the sin of Cain and appropriating God's warning as a threat to protect himself:

> Lamech said to his wives, "Adah and Zillah, listen to me; wives of Lamech, hear my words. I have killed a man for wounding me, a young man for injuring me. If Cain is avenged seven times, then Lamech seventy-seven times." (Genesis 4:23-24).

---

[6] "Avon," The Bible Project, https://www.youtube.com/watch?v=w1zkwkI9oAw&list=PLH0Szn1yYNeclOdfwWBawnNT5ZkGFHxBf&index=14&t=182s.

Genesis 4 shows us that even when God gave humans an invitation to repent and change, they didn't take it, but only fell deeper in bondage to sin and its punishment of destructive consequences. This pattern continued until "every inclination of the thoughts of the human heart was only evil all the time" and the earth became so corrupt and full of violence that God "regretted that he had made human beings on the earth" (Genesis 6:5-6).

ADDICTED TO CONTROL

The progression of human behavior we see in Genesis 3-6 is exactly what Paul describes in detail in Romans 1:

> For God in heaven unveils his holy anger breaking forth against every form of sin, both toward ungodliness that lives in hearts and evil actions. For the wickedness of humanity deliberately smothers the truth and keeps people from acknowledging the truth about God. In reality, the truth of God is known instinctively, for God has embedded this knowledge inside every human heart. Opposition to truth cannot be excused on the basis of ignorance, because from the creation of the world, the invisible qualities of God's nature have been made visible, such as his eternal power and transcendence. He has made his wonderful attributes easily perceived, for seeing the visible makes us understand the invisible. So then, this leaves everyone without excuse. Throughout human history the fingerprints of God were upon them, yet they refused to honor him as God or even be thankful for his kindness. Instead, they entertained corrupt and foolish thoughts about what God was like. This left them with nothing but misguided hearts, steeped in moral darkness. Although claiming to be super-intelligent, they were in fact shal-

> low fools. For only a fool would trade the unfading splendor of the immortal God to worship the fading image of other humans, idols made to look like people, animals, birds, and even creeping reptiles! This is why God lifted off his restraining hand and let them have full expression of their sinful and shameful desires . . . God gave them over to their own disgraceful and vile passions . . . And because they thought it was worthless to embrace the true knowledge of God, God gave them over to a worthless mind-set, to break all rules of proper conduct. Their sinful lives became full of every kind of evil, wicked schemes, greed, and cruelty. (Romans 1:18-24, 26, 28-29 TPT)

This passage gets right to the heart of what is wrong with us and how we've ended up in the state we're in. First, the truth of who God really is, His nature and character, is not a secret in our world. God is good, powerful, and kind. We just refuse to see and believe it. We cling to the enemy's false narrative about who He is and fall into spiritual blindness. This leads us into idolatry—putting ourselves in the place of God.

The phrase "because they thought it was worthless to embrace the true knowledge of God, God gave them over to a worthless mind-set" gives us the point of origin for the core belief of the punishment paradigm: "My flaws and failures make me *unworthy* of love, belonging, and connection. I deserve disconnection and punishment. So does everyone else with flaws and failures." God is the supreme value of the universe, from which everything He created derives its value. Our unwillingness to honor His worth, and our attempt to place other things (including ourselves) in that place of supreme value, is what introduced shame, the painful belief in our own unworthiness.

This shame established the fear of punishment, with its goal of self-preservation, as the driving motive of our hearts. One of the ways

Scripture helps us recognize the fear of punishment is by contrasting it with another type of fear called "the fear of the Lord." The fear of the Lord is the opposite of the fear of punishment. Its goal is protecting connection, not pursuing self-preservation, and nowhere does it use punishment as a strategy to achieve that goal. The fear of the Lord leads us toward God, not away from Him. The fear of punishment, however, leads us either to run from God or to try to maintain a safe distance from Him. This always involves the double-edged dance of trying to avoid punishment ourselves while also trying to leverage it as a tool of control and self-protection toward others. Like Adam and Eve, and like Cain, we try to hide and cover ourselves while painting targets of blame, anger, and retribution on others.

Above all, the fear of God is a response to the truth of God's character, while the fear of punishment is driven by the enemy's lies. This is why the fear of punishment leads us to continue assassinating God's character by projecting our bad motives and behavior on to Him. Classically in our imaginations, He is either an absent, abandoning God who can't be bothered to get involved with the messy dealings of sinful man, or when He does get involved, it is as an angry Judge and Punisher. Through the lens of our fear, we see Him doing the same dance of avoiding and avenging that we ourselves do. And we use this false caricature of God to justify both our sinning and our punishment.

What's really happening is another story, however. God is not sitting in heaven turning a blind eye to our sin or playing tit for tat, trying to intimidate us into good behavior. According to Paul, God's "holy anger" is expressed by "lifting off His restraining hand" and "giving us over" to the consequences of our idolatry, allowing us to fall in a downward spiral of depravity that disintegrates and destroys our humanity. He "punishes" by honoring the free will He gave us—letting us dig our own pit and then fall into it. This implies that His default position is actually one of restraining—of working with us in ways that serve to hold back sin and its consequences. And as the story continues, we see the lengths to which God will go to rescue us from the pit of sin and punishment into which we'd fallen.

Anyone who has been in a relationship with an addict knows what it's like to watch a person who seems dead-set on their own destruction. Many times, the only thing to do is to let the person drive themselves to rock bottom. This is exactly what Paul is describing at the end of Romans 1—except he's talking about the whole human race. In the last chapter I stated that we are addicted to punishment, but now we see this is just part of the picture of our true spiritual addiction. What we are really addicted to is trying to be our own gods. We want to make the rules. We want to be in control. We want to make the messes we want, and then we want to dictate the terms by which they are cleaned up—or not.

Among the endless examples I could cite of how our human addiction to punishment plays out in our current culture, I'll mention one here that we easily ignore and minimize—entertainment. A culture's entertainment always reflects our deepest core values and agreements. Our most popular movies, sports, and video games are filled with expressions of violent punishment of those who "deserve" it. The biggest sporting events, such as the NFL, NHL, UFC, or boxing must find new levels of punishing interaction or lose ratings. Our movies and TV shows need more deaths, gore, blood, and vengeance or they will struggle at the box office. Many video games are the new training ground for spectacular levels of disrespectful human interactions among our very young impressionable, unsupervised next generation. It's as though our psyche cries out for more supply and severity of disrespectful treatment of one another.

However, like all addicts, the more we feed our appetite for punishment—which is our appetite for control—the more we end up being controlled. The more we use punishment as a tool to feel powerful, the more the fear of punishment runs our lives. And God is willing to let us hit rock bottom, to let us experience firsthand just what awful rulers of the planet, or of our own lives, we are without Him.

But He doesn't leave us there. Over centuries, He executes a large-scale plan to break us out of the idolatry, shame, and destruction of the punishment paradigm and back to a place of trust and connection with Him, ourselves, and one another. As we will see in the next chapter, the entire Old Testament is a story of God choosing a people whom He will not let go. While they go their own way, He will reposition Himself again and again to rebuild a connection with His people, regardless of what they do towards Him.

SECTION II

OUR CALL TO THE COVENANT OF LOVE

CHAPTER 4

THE COVENANT-MAKING GOD

"Hey, Danny, I need your help." By the sound of his shaking voice, my friend Jerry was deeply upset about something.

"What's going on?" I asked.

"Maria spent the night at her friend Becky's last night. Apparently, they found a bottle of vodka, got drunk, and decided to go over to Becky's neighbor's house and throw his lawn furniture in his pool. The reason I found out is that the neighbor happens to be my boss. I got a call from him telling me what the girls did right after Maria came home this morning. I just tried to talk to her and it didn't go well. I need you to tell me what to do."

"Okay, man, I'm coming over," I said. "I can hear that you're pretty angry about this. Let's talk about how you can show her your broken heart instead of your anger."

"Thanks, Danny . . ." Jerry sounded unsure. "I'll see you soon."

When I got to Jerry's, he admitted that he had already shown punishing anger toward his fifteen-year-old daughter. After his boss had called, he'd gone into her room holding his mug of morning coffee and asked her, "So how did it feel to be drunk?" Maria had looked him in the face and said, “It felt great. I really liked it.” Jerry was not prepared for that answer. He already felt powerless and humiliated, and now he was hurt that she didn’t feel any desire to apologize or change her behavior. Enraged, he had flung his coffee mug across the room and shattered her closet mirror.

Jerry regretted that decision, but was still hung up on how to get his daughter under control. I encouraged him to repent and clean up his mess with his daughter. Sadly, the damage was done. His punishing anger didn’t just discourage Maria from changing, it hardened her heart towards him. She spun hard into a teenage rebellion that lasted until she left home. Many years passed before father and daughter were able to repair their connection.

To this day, many people think of God—especially the way He is portrayed in the Old Testament—as an angry and punishing dad like my friend. Only instead of throwing coffee cups into mirrors, He sends floods, fire, disease, and famine to destroy rebellious people who violate His holiness.

When we try to put Him in the matrix of the punishment paradigm, however, it quickly becomes clear that He doesn’t fit. God’s actions are not motivated by shame or the fear of punishment. He is not trying to protect His own holiness in divine self-preservation. He is not insecure, controlling, or vindictive. So, when we look at the incidents in the Bible where God “punishes” people, we need to be careful not to project our own punishment paradigm thinking on to Him and learn to understand the significance of His behavior in the framework of the biblical narrative. As we’ll see in this chapter and the next, the full arc of the story of the Bible shows us that God’s entire mission in human history is to set us free from the punishment paradigm and lead us into a completely new, punishment-free relational paradigm with Him, ourselves, and others.

JUST ONE "RESET"

Let's pick up the story of the Bible where we left off, just after Cain initiates his legacy of murder and retribution in his family line in Genesis 4. When we get to Genesis 6, we learn that this legacy has continued and multiplied throughout the human race, covering the earth with violence (Genesis 6:13). Apparently, with no divine intervention to stop the exponential devastation of *avon*—sin and its consequences—people have become so corrupt that "every inclination of the thoughts of the human heart is only evil all the time" (Genesis 6:5). This is how the world ends up when God "punishes" humanity by turning them over to the project of trying to be their own gods and defining good and evil for themselves. There is no justice, righteousness, or mercy, only unrestrained evil, violence, and corruption.

The first thing Scripture tells us about God's response to this state of affairs on His planet is not what He did, but what He *felt*: "And the LORD was sorry that He had made man on the earth, and He was grieved in His heart." (Genesis 6:6 NKJV). His response to an earth filled with corruption and violence—the Flood—was motivated not by punishing anger or vindictiveness, but by sadness. Humanity was already being punished by its own depravity. Wiping the slate clean by cleansing the earth was not about punishing people, but about ending the vicious cycles of punishment in which they were bound and giving humanity a fresh start. This is why He didn't destroy humanity completely, but started over with Noah and his family.

However, though Noah was called "righteous," he was not immune to sin. God Himself declared after the Flood that "every inclination of the human heart is evil from childhood" (Genesis 8:21). This meant that this new human race would still have the old problems and inevitably end up creating the same legacy of corruption, wickedness, and violence down the road. However, God didn't say, "Well, I guess I'll just wipe everyone out and start over every time things get bad enough." Our society loves to entertain apocalyptic fantasies about the world being wiped clean by nuclear war or natural disasters. Many people concerned with climate change have predicted all kinds of catastrophic events in the future that will drastically reduce the population and "reset" the planet. But after the Flood, God established that He wouldn't work with us like that. Instead, He promised Noah that He would never flood the earth again, and initiated a new chapter in the story, a chapter in which He would begin to intervene and engage in human affairs in a different way.

FOUR COVENANTS

> I am going to bring floodwaters on the earth to destroy all life under the heavens, every creature that has the breath of life in it. Everything on earth will perish. But I will establish my covenant with you, and you will enter the ark—you and your sons and your wife and your sons' wives with you. (Genesis 6:17-18)

God's words to Noah mark the first place in the Bible where the word "covenant" appears. In ancient Near Eastern culture, covenants were legal partnerships—primarily between kings or rulers—that typically involved a set of promises and commitments and were solemnized through some form of "cutting" ceremony or covenant meal.[7] The Old Testament records four main covenants that God initiates with humans:

Covenant 1: God and Noah

Covenant 2: God and Abraham

Covenant 3: God and Moses/the people of Israel

Covenant 4: God and David

---

[7] The Hebrew word for covenant, *beriyth*, comes from *bara*, "to cut, to eat." (Strong's H1285)

Each covenant adds to a progressive revelation of God's plan to restore fallen humanity and our connection with Him. The first covenant with Noah consists simply of a promise and a sign—the rainbow stands as a lasting reminder that God will never flood the earth again (Genesis 9:9-17). God requires nothing from Noah and his family on their side of the partnership, though He does command them to uphold the value of humans being made in the image of God:

> And for your lifeblood I will surely demand an accounting. I will demand an accounting from every animal. And from each human being, too, I will demand an accounting for the life of another human being. Whoever sheds human blood, by humans shall their blood be shed; for in the image of God has God made mankind. (Genesis 9:5-6)

True to His word, when Noah's descendants conspire yet again to be their own gods and make a name for themselves by building the tower of Babel, God does not destroy them, but scatters them by confusing their languages. After this scattering, God chooses Abram as a covenant partner. He promises to give Abram an heir and many descendants, who will possess the land of Canaan. For the first covenant-making ceremony, God has Abram cut animals in half and passes between them as He declares His promise to give the land of Canaan to his descendants (Genesis 15:17-21). Passing between the pieces symbolically announced, "If I fail to keep my covenant promises, let what has been done to these animals be done to me." God was sending the message to Abram, "There's nothing you can do to be disqualified from this covenant. I take full responsibility for these promises, and you can be absolutely sure I will do what I've said."

Despite God's assurances, Abram attempts fulfill God's covenant promises on his own terms by having a son with his female slave. However, when God shows up to keep His promise, He issues no correction or punishment to Abram, but initiates another covenant ceremony in which He changes Abram's name to Abraham, promising to make him a father of many nations and establish His covenant with all of Abraham's descendants, beginning with his future son, Isaac (Genesis 17:1-21). This time, the "cutting" does not happen to the animals, but to Abraham's own flesh through the act of circumcision—a sign that every child born through Abraham from then on would belong to this everlasting covenant. Passing this sign on to each generation seems to be the only thing God requires of Abraham on his end of the covenant. God later appears to Isaac, and then to Isaac's son, Jacob, whose name He changes to Israel, to renew His covenant promises with them (see Genesis 26:3-4, 24, 28:13-15, 35:10-12).

As in Noah's story, punishment doesn't really appear at all in Abraham's covenant history with God, though the tales of the four generations of this family in Genesis 12-50 contain *a lot* of sinful messes. Abraham lies about his wife Sarah to protect himself, calling her his sister, and his son Isaac later does the same with his wife Rebekah. Abraham and Sarah conspire to sexually use Hagar to get a son. Rebekah and Jacob connive in deceiving Isaac and cheating Esau of his blessing. And Jacob's sons murder the men of an entire city to avenge their sister and sell their brother Joseph into slavery. These "fathers of the faith" were full of self-preservation, control, manipulation, fear, deceit, and retribution, but not once did God step in to judge or punish them. He simply pursued relationship with them faithfully over the years, made huge promises to them, and protected and blessed them. The main purpose of this covenant was to demonstrate God's heart to form a covenant family for Himself.

THE OLD COVENANT—EXPOSING HARD HEARTS

The book of Exodus opens with Abraham's descendants falling into slavery in Egypt and languishing for four hundred years under the harsh oppression of hard-hearted Pharaoh. God sends Moses to liberate them, confronting the gods and armies of Egypt in dramatic fashion and leading the people out under the atoning blood of the Passover lamb and the baptismal waters of the Red Sea (see 1 Corinthians 10:2). Moses then brings the people to Mount Sinai for another covenant ceremony. This covenant is different than those with Noah and Abraham in a couple key respects. First, God is inviting not one man, or even a family, but an entire nation to enter a covenant partnership with Him. Second, He wants them to play a specific, much more complex role in this partnership. Thus, He has some specific requirements He needs them to fulfill:

> Then Moses went up to God, and the LORD called to him from the mountain and said, "This is what you are to say to the descendants of Jacob and what you are to tell the people of Israel: 'You yourselves have seen what I did to Egypt, and how I carried you on eagles' wings and brought you to myself. Now if you obey me fully and keep my covenant, then out of all nations you will be my treasured possession. Although the whole earth is mine, you will be for me a kingdom of priests and a holy nation.' These are the words you are to speak to the Israelites." (Exodus 19:3-6)

God's heart and intention for His covenant partners was they would be absolutely special to Him and set apart from all other people on earth. He also wanted them to be His priests—to minister to Him and be His representatives to the rest of the world. This was a much higher calling than what He had asked of Abraham, Isaac, and Jacob, who had done no more than receive God's promises and blessings and perform a few notable acts of obedience to His instructions. Now God wanted an entire nation to walk in relationship with Him and show the rest of the world what He was like.

This calling represented a steep learning curve for people who had been brought up as slaves in a pagan culture and had only just been introduced to the LORD. The only way it could work is if they were willing to listen and obey His instructions for how to fulfill their end of the covenant. This was the purpose for this meeting at Sinai—to lay out God's vision for their covenant culture as His people and initiate this brand-new way of life in relationship with Him.

There is a powerful moment early in this covenant-making process that sets the tone for how it unfolds. After the people say yes to God's invitation to be His "treasured possession," "kingdom of priests," and "holy nation," Moses instructs them to prepare to witness the conversation in which God will deliver His covenant instructions. They purify themselves, approach the mountain, and watch in awe as God's presence descends with fire, lightning, smoke, and trumpet blasts:

> Now all the people witnessed the thunderings, the lightning flashes, the sound of the trumpet, and the mountain smoking; and when the people saw [it], they trembled and stood afar off. Then they said to Moses, "You speak with us, and we will hear; but let not God speak with us, lest we die." And Moses said to the people, "*Do not fear; for God has come to test you, and that His fear may be before you, so that you may not sin.*" (Exodus 20:18-21, NKJV emphasis added)

At first glance, Moses' command appears to be a contradiction in terms. He tells them not to fear because God wants His fear to be before them. But here in one verse we see the two types of fear contrasted throughout the Scriptures—the fear of punishment that leads us to put distance from ourselves and God, and the fear of God that keeps us from sinning—that is, from violating connection with Him, ourselves, and others. The fear of punishment drives the punishment paradigm, while the fear of God, which is actually a dimension of love, drives God's relational covenant paradigm.

From the very beginning, we see that God is after the *hearts* of His people. This is where the fundamental change needs to happen to bring them out of their old slavery mindset into the relational culture He wants to establish with them. However, as the story unfolds, we see again and again that God's people do not make this internal shift from the fear of punishment to the fear of God. Their hearts don't change. Almost immediately after they tell Moses, "All that the LORD has said we will do, and be obedient" (Exodus 24:7-8 NKJV), they break the first two commandments God gave them by building and worshipping an idol—the beginning of the pattern they will repeat for thousands of years.

The conversation God has with Moses on the mountain while the Israelites are down below worshipping the golden calf exposes the unique situation in which God has put Himself by making a covenant with a people who will break that covenant again and again and again. "'I have seen these people,' the LORD said to Moses, 'and they are a stiff-necked people'" (Exodus 32:9). The word "stiff-necked" means "hard" or "harsh"—it's the same word used earlier in Exodus to describe the "harsh" labor the Israelites were subjected to and the "hard" heart of Pharaoh in opposing God.[8] In the confrontation with the ten plagues, God gave Pharaoh multiple opportunities to repent, but each time Pharaoh hardened his heart—until God finally turned Pharaoh over to that state permanently.[9] Now the story suggests that the Israelites will follow the same trajectory of resisting God leading to their own destruction.

---

[8] "H7186 - qasheh - Strong's Hebrew Lexicon (NIV)." Blue Letter Bible. Accessed 24 Jul, 2019. https://www.blueletterbible.org//lang/lexicon/lexicon.cfm?Strongs=H7186&t=NIV

[9] In Genesis 15 when God makes the covenant with Abram, He speaks to Abram in a dream and tells him that his descendants will be enslaved and mistreated for four hundred years, but that God will "punish" the nation that enslaved them and bring

Yet God allows Moses, representing Israel's end of the covenant, to plead their case and ask Him to stay in relationship with them for the sake of His covenant with Abraham, Isaac, and Jacob. The Lord "[relents and does] not bring on his people the disaster he had threatened" (Exodus 32:14). However, He does promise that He will hold His people accountable for their sins—"when the time comes for me to punish, I will punish them for their sin" (Exodus 32:34). This combined response of mercy and justice demonstrates what God later declares to Moses when He hides him in the rock and declares His name—the description of His nature—as He passes by:

> And he passed in front of Moses, proclaiming, "The LORD, the LORD, the compassionate and gracious God, slow to anger, abounding in love and faithfulness, maintaining love to thousands, and forgiving wickedness, rebellion and sin. Yet he does not leave the guilty unpunished; he punishes the children and their children for the sin of the parents to the third and fourth generation." (Exodus 34:6-7)

This statement expresses the fundamental tension God must navigate as a good God who is faithful to uphold His end of the covenant, and to hold His covenant partners accountable for their end. His heart toward His people is full of love, compassion, and grace. Yet if He does not hold them accountable when they betray their covenant, He ceases to be a faithful covenant partner Himself. Holding the guilty accountable is an expression of covenant love. And there are two ways He can respond to the guilty: forgiveness and punishment.

---

them out. He does this by "turning Pharaoh over" to his hard heart—when Pharaoh refuses to repent, God fixes him in that unrepentant state and allows him to play into his own destruction.

God is using this relational dilemma with Israel to reveal the nature of His dilemma with all of humanity. His relationship with humans from the beginning was covenantal—a partnership with guidelines, responsibilities, and blessings. He created humans in His image and appointed us as rulers of creation, which makes Him responsible for giving us that authority and for dealing with us when we abuse it. When we betray our relationships with God, ourselves, and others through sin, we incur a spiritual debt, and there is only one way that debt can be satisfied. Either we, the person who incurred the debt, must repay it—that is, be punished—or God, the person to whom it is owed, must forgive it—that is, cover the payment Himself. God, in His goodness, is both merciful and just because He does not abandon His responsibility to keep us accountable in our relationship with Him. His nature demands that He deal with our sinful betrayal, either by forgiveness or punishment.

This is the point where the story of Scripture begins to raise some important questions. First, under what conditions can God forgive sins—what does "covering the payment" actually involve? And second, what is God's heart and goal in dealing with sin? Does He want to punish or forgive? What kind of relationship does He want to have with His people?

The purpose of the Book of the Covenant—which we typically think of as just a long list of rules—was to answer these questions and help God's covenant partners understand how He wanted to make things work between them. The overall message of the laws Moses received on the mountain was that sinless, holy God wanted a faithful, loving connection with a sinful people. This is why He teaches them what sin is (moral purity laws), gives them a way for atoning for their sin through substitutionary sacrifices so He can forgive them (sacrificial laws), and establishes a worship center (Tabernacle) and cultural practices that regularly remind them of His holiness and the holy life to which He has called them (ceremonial/ritual purity laws). All of this instruction (*torah*) sent the message that God was committed to walk in relationship with His people. He was inviting them into a covenant culture where they had the opportunity to learn to walk uprightly before Him and be restored when they sinned, rather than be destroyed.

Despite saying yes to God's covenant invitation, however, Israel demonstrates again and again that they do not have the same goal of connection with God. They continue to live up to their reputation as a "stiff-necked" people, requiring God to live up to His name as a punisher of sin. In that first generation alone, they complain, disobey, and rebel on multiple occasions, prompting God to punish the guilty and unrepentant. In the end, their refusal to walk faithfully with God leaves them condemned to wander in the wilderness till they die. God then turns His attention to the next generation, offering them the chance to learn from their parents' failures and choose to be faithful where they were not.

DAVID'S DESCENDANT AND THE NEW COVENANT

For the next few millennia, Israel follows the same pattern in their covenant with God. Joshua takes the baton from Moses and leads a faithful generation into the Promised Land. After he is gone, the people fall into idolatry and break their covenant, which leads them, just as God had warned them, into oppression by their enemies. Eventually, they cry out to God and He raises up judges to deliver the people and bring them back to covenant faithfulness, but each time their seasons of success give way to seasons of betrayal.

Later, God appoints kings to lead Israel, the most famous of whom is David, the man "after His own heart" (1 Samuel 13:14). Though David makes some of the biggest messes in the Bible, he stands out as one whose heart was *not* hard toward God. Unlike King Saul, David repents when confronted with his sin. Yes, he does experience some pretty devastating consequences for his sin—his first son with Bathsheba dies, and two of his other sons, Amnon and Absalom, later die after wreaking havoc in the family and nation. Yet David is not removed from his position and later killed as Saul was. Instead of punishing him, God makes a covenant with him, promising to establish David's line and raise up a descendant to sit on his throne forever:

> "I declare to you that the LORD will build a house for you: When your days are over and you go to be with your ancestors, I will raise up your offspring to succeed you, one of your own sons, and I will establish his kingdom. He is the one who will build a house for me, and I will establish his throne forever. I will be his father, and he will be my son. I will never take my love away from him, as I took it away from your predecessor. I will set him over my house and my kingdom forever; his throne will be established forever." (1 Chronicles 17:10-14)

David's son Solomon takes the throne and later builds God a house—the Temple—making it look briefly like he could be the one to fulfill this promise. But though he is the one who writes the book of Proverbs acknowledging that "the fear of the Lord is the beginning of wisdom" (Proverbs 9:10), Solomon's heart is seduced away from the love of God through his foreign wives and he leads the nation back into idolatry. From that point on, Israel's kings (with a few exceptions) fail to lead the people in covenant faithfulness, and eventually God's people end up in exile. The Old Testament ends as God is restoring a remnant to the land, but there seems to be no guarantee that Israel won't break their covenant again. Its final words speak of God sending a prophet to "turn the hearts" of the generations (Malachi 4:6), but at this point, nothing we see in the Bible has brought about lasting covenant faithfulness in the hearts of God's people.

It's very tempting to read human failure as the dominant theme of the Old Testament. Every time God attempts to walk with humans in a covenant relationship, we end up falling for the old temptation to be our own gods, hardening our hearts against Him, and putting Him in the position where He must deal with our betrayal. But God is the hero of the Bible, not us. The Bible is the story of His covenant faithfulness, not our treachery. He has never once turned His love off toward us or stopped pursuing connection with us. In His covenant history, we see a progressive revelation of how He sees and defines the problem that keeps us from the relationship He desires to have with us—and the solution He has prepared for that problem.

Two big Old Testament promises point to this solution. First, God declares through the prophets Ezekiel and Jeremiah that He plans to make a new covenant with His people—a covenant in which all sin is forgiven, and where God puts a new heart and spirit within us:

> "Behold, the days are coming, says the LORD, when I will make a new covenant with the house of Israel and with the house of Judah—not according to the covenant that I made with their fathers in the day [that] I took them by the hand to lead them out of the land of Egypt, My covenant which they broke, though I was a husband to them, says the LORD . . . I will put My law in their minds, and write it on their hearts; and I will be their God, and they shall be My people. No more shall every man teach his neighbor, and every man his brother, saying, 'Know the LORD,' for they all shall know Me, from the least of them to the greatest of them, says the LORD. For I will forgive their iniquity, and their sin I will remember no more." (Jeremiah 31:31-34 NKJV)

> "I will give you a new heart and put a new spirit within you; I will take the heart of stone out of your flesh and give you a heart of flesh. I will put My Spirit within you and cause you to walk in My statutes, and you will keep My judgments and do [them]. (Ezekiel 36:26-27 NKJV)

The implication here is clear—the problem with the old covenant lay in the hearts of people. A heart of flesh—a heart connected to the Spirit of life—is soft, responsive, trusting, and willing to listen. A heart of stone resists connection with the Spirit. It is seduced, deceived, and intimidated by other voices and ultimately turns in on itself. A hard heart is what keeps us locked in the unholy fear and self-preservation of the punishment paradigm, which is the matrix of sin. God, who is the only rightful punisher of sin in the universe, and who does punish it as an act of covenant faithfulness, is not interested in keeping sinful humanity in a state where they will continuously deserve punishment. He intends to deal with the sin problem, and therefore the punishment problem, once and for all.

The second promise is that the true Son of David, the Messiah, will come to rescue and lead the people of God in covenant faithfulness. Unlike Solomon, who abandoned the covenant and the fear of the Lord, this faithful king will walk in the Spirit and delight in the fear of the Lord:

> A shoot will come up from the stump of Jesse; from his roots a Branch will bear fruit. The Spirit of the LORD will rest on him—the Spirit of wisdom and of understanding, the Spirit of counsel and of might, the Spirit of the knowledge and fear of the LORD—and he will delight in the fear of the LORD. (Isaiah 11:1-3)

Isaiah later predicted that this king would also be the suffering servant who would carry away the sins of the people:

> Surely he took up our pain and bore our suffering, yet we considered him punished by God, stricken by him, and afflicted. But he was pierced for our transgressions, he was crushed for our iniquities; the punishment that brought us peace was on him,

> and by his wounds we are healed. We all, like sheep, have gone astray, each of us has turned to our own way; and the LORD has laid on him the iniquity of us all. (Isaiah 53:4-6)

In the next chapter, we will look at how Jesus fulfilled these great promises and ushered in God's epic solution to the problem keeping us from walking in unbroken connection with Him.

CHAPTER 5

THE NEW COVENANT

God's covenant-making history with humans culminates in a stunning way. True to the prophecies He spoke through Ezekiel and Jeremiah, God establishes a *new* covenant, and the most important and dramatically different thing is *who* He makes this covenant with. Both of those prophecies point to the arrival of a new breed of humans on the planet—humans who will know the Lord, have His law written on their hearts, have hearts of flesh and not of stone, and have the Spirit of God in them. This humanity 2.0 will come into being because God "will forgive their iniquity, and their sin [He] will remember no more" (Jeremiah 31:34)—that is, He will bring about a relationship in which sin and its consequences—punishment—have been permanently done away with through His forgiveness. In this new covenant, forgiveness will open the door to our total transformation and bring us out of the punishment paradigm for good.

The central theme of the New Testament is that this new human race arrived on earth with the birth of Jesus Christ. He is the Second and Last Adam (1 Corinthians 15:45), "the image of the invisible God, the firstborn over all creation" (Colossians 1:15). The great mystery of His identity is that He is both fully human and fully God, which means that in Him, we see both who we were created to be, and who God truly is.

We see the faithful Son of Man who perfectly fulfills our human side of covenant with God, living out not only the letter of the Law, but its heart to honor and protect connection with God, self, and others. We also see the faithful Son of God who perfectly reveals the heart of the Father for us, displaying the covenant partnership God has longed to have with us from the beginning. Through Jesus, a covenant becomes possible that never was before—a covenant between the Father and the Son, and between the Father and the new human race that is *in* the Son.

A NEW WAY TO DEAL WITH SINNERS

In revealing the Father, Jesus systematically confronted and exposed humanity's false views of God—in particular, the view of God as a punisher who endorses the human punishment paradigm—while revealing His plan to eliminate the punishment paradigm by forgiving sin. For example, instead of participating in the traditional social punishments of the day towards sinners, tax collectors, the ethnically impure, and others considered to be "unclean" or "outsiders"—all of which were justified in the culture on religious grounds—He welcomed them, ate with them, and numbered them among His followers. He rebuked His disciples when they suggested He "call down fire" on a Samaritan village that didn't welcome Him (Luke 9:52-56). And in what is surely one of the most dramatic scenes in the New Testament, He refused to participate in punishment when a group of Pharisees brought Him a woman caught in adultery:

> At dawn he appeared again in the temple courts, where all the people gathered around him, and he sat down to teach them. The teachers of the law and the Pharisees brought in a woman caught in adultery. They made her stand before the group and said to Jesus, "Teacher, this woman was caught in the act of adultery. In the Law Moses commanded us to stone such women. Now what do you say?" They were using this question as a trap,

> in order to have a basis for accusing him. But Jesus bent down and started to write on the ground with his finger. When they kept on questioning him, he straightened up and said to them, "Let any one of you who is without sin be the first to throw a stone at her." Again he stooped down and wrote on the ground. At this, those who heard began to go away one at a time, the older ones first, until only Jesus was left, with the woman still standing there. Jesus straightened up and asked her, "Woman, where are they? Has no one condemned you?" "No one, sir," she said. "Then neither do I condemn you," Jesus declared. "Go now and leave your life of sin." (John 8:2-11)

Here we see a sinner, her punishers, who are also sinners, and the sinless Son of God, who alone has the true right to punish sin and hold sinners accountable. In one sentence, Jesus fully de-authorizes the punishers by reminding them that they are, in fact, on the same footing as the sinner they want to punish. In the next sentence, Jesus tells that sinner, "Neither am I your punisher." After establishing that there are no punishers in sight, He commissions the sinner to a life of freedom from sin. The message was clear. When the Pharisees said, "Here's how Moses told us to deal with sinners," Jesus responded, "We're not doing it that way anymore. I'm ushering in a new paradigm where sinners aren't punished but offered a way out of their sinful lifestyle."

What was this new paradigm, and how did Jesus—the One who came not to abolish what Moses and the Prophets had written, but to fulfill it—usher it in?

FORGIVENESS REQUIRES AN OFFERING

God told Moses that He responds to sin in two ways—He "[forgives] wickedness, rebellion and sin . . . [and] does not leave the guilty unpunished" (Exodus 34:7). His first and primary action toward sin is to forgive it as an expression of covenant love and faithfulness—this is how He stays in relationship with sinful people. But this doesn't mean that He lets people off the hook. The reality of sin and its punishment must be dealt with. This is not a contradiction in God's character; it's an invitation to understand sin, punishment, and what is required for God to forgive sin.

The Hebrew word for "forgive"—*nasa'*—clues us in to how forgiveness works. It means "to lift, bear up, carry, take."[10] When God forgives us, He lifts the burden of our sin and carries it away. Dr. Tim Mackie explains:

> "Carrying *avon*" [sin or iniquity] is the common Hebrew phrase for God's forgiveness. Like Psalm 32, where the poet says, "I didn't hide my *avon*, but confessed it, and You carried the *avon* of my sin." This is actually shocking if you stop and think about it. God forgives people by taking responsibility for their *avon*.[11]

If you remember, *avon* encompasses both sin and its punishment. The idea of God carrying our *avon* means that He takes the punishment for sin on Himself. This is what it means for Him to forgive, a reality symbolized for centuries through Israel's sacrificial system. In addition to sacrifices people made for their own sins, each year the priests offered two goats as sacrifices for the sins of the entire nation on the Day of Atonement. One goat was slaughtered and its blood sprinkled on the cover (the "mercy seat" or "atonement cover") of the Ark of the Covenant. The other goat became the scapegoat—the one on which the high

[10] https://www.blueletterbible.org/lang/lexicon/lexicon.cfm?Strongs=H5375&t=NIV
[11] "Avon," The Bible Project, https://www.youtube.com/watch?v=w1zkwkI9oAw&list=PLH0Szn1yYNeclOdfwWBawnNT5ZkGFHxBf&index=14&t=182s.

priest would lay his hands to impart the sins of the nation, then send off into the wilderness to carry the sins away. Together, the two goats created a picture of God covering the sin of His people through a sacrifice of blood (life) and bearing it away from them—both separating them from their mess and cleaning it up.

This system was provisional, however—the life of an animal could never fully atone for human sin, but only remind people that God was showing mercy because He had a plan to cover and carry away their sins in the future by other means. As the fall of the kingdoms of Judah and Israel approached, during which the first Temple and its sacrificial system were destroyed, God revealed that He would be sending a "righteous servant" to become an "offering for sin":

> He was despised and rejected by mankind, a man of suffering, and familiar with pain . . . Surely he took up our pain and bore our suffering, yet we considered him *punished* by God, stricken by him, and afflicted. But he was pierced for our transgressions, he was crushed for our iniquities; the *punishment* that brought us peace was on him, and by his wounds we are healed. We all, like sheep, have gone astray, each of us has turned to our own way; and the LORD has laid on him the iniquity of us all . . . for the transgression of my people he was *punished* . . . and though the LORD makes his life an offering for sin, he will see his offspring and prolong his days, and the will of the LORD will prosper in his hand. After he has suffered, he will see the light of life and be satisfied; by his knowledge my righteous servant will justify many, and he will bear their iniquities . . . he poured out his life unto death, and was numbered with the transgressors. For he bore the sin of many, and made intercession for the transgressors. (Isaiah 53:3-12)

In describing how this "righteous servant" will cover and bear away the burden of sin, Isaiah's words bring out the nuances of sin's punishment. This Servant will not simply be killed—He will endure pain, suffering, piercing, crushing, and wounds. Sin brings disintegration of spirit, soul, body, and relationships. Its punishment is the fracturing and loss of *shalom*—the relational wholeness with God, ourselves, each other, and the earth in which we were designed to live and thrive. The experience of this disintegration and brokenness in and around us is nothing less than painful, terrifying, tormenting, and crushing, and it is this experience that this Servant will take on for us—to the point of his own destruction.

The greater revelation Jesus unveiled was that He, the promised Servant, was actually God Himself, come in the flesh. One of the things that most shocked Jesus' audience during His ministry was His audacity to tell people, "Your sins are forgiven." The teachers of the law who heard Him say this knew He was claiming to be equal with God. Then again, Jesus' disciples, who were convinced that He *was* the Son of God, were equally shocked—and devastated—when He willingly allowed Himself to be betrayed, arrested, slandered, beaten, pierced, mocked, scourged, crushed, and executed on one of the most terrible human instruments of torture and shame. It took years before they finally began to connect the dots—that when Jesus had told someone their sins were forgiven, He had done so in the knowledge that He would shortly become the promised "offering for sin" that would enable God to fully and finally forgive the sin of humanity once and for all. God the Son had been working with God the Father to execute their plan to defeat and abolish sin, punishment, and death, and deliver us from the kingdom of darkness into the kingdom of the Son.

WHO PUNISHED JESUS?

Many books have been written unpacking the significance of Christ's suffering and death and how His sacrifice satisfied the wrath of

God toward sin. This subject brings up age-old questions—Doesn't the idea of the Father punishing Jesus sound like divine child abuse? Why would a loving God kill His own Son? If God is so loving, why is He so full of wrath? Does He really condemn people to eternal punishment in hell?

Before we look at these questions and what happened through the crucifixion at the divine level, it's important to pay attention to the human level. The story we read in the Gospels makes two things perfectly clear: 1) humans punished and killed Jesus, and 2) He willingly allowed it to happen. Specifically, it was the religious leaders of the day—the custodians of the old covenant— who plotted and instigated Jesus' punishment. Why did those who diligently studied the Law and the Prophets, and should have been most ready to receive the promised Messiah, end up rejecting and crucifying Him? Jesus Himself told us why. He knew exactly who would plot His execution and for what reason, and boldly said so to their faces.

Two of Jesus' parables pinpoint why the religious leaders felt so threatened and enraged by Jesus that they decided to put Him down. The first is His parable about the owner of a vineyard who sent servant after servant to collect on the harvest of his land. Each time, the tenants who worked the land beat the servants and sent them away empty-handed. Finally, the owner sent his son to the tenants, hoping that they would finally respond to him with respect. "But when the tenants saw the son, they said to each other, 'This is the heir. Come, let's kill him and take his inheritance.' So they took him and threw him out of the vineyard and killed him" (Matthew 21:38-39).

The symbolism was clear to Jesus' audience—He was the son and the religious leaders were the rebellious tenants who wanted to kill Him. "When the chief priests and the Pharisees heard Jesus' parables, they knew he was talking about them" (Matthew 21:45). And what was the Son's "inheritance"? It was His spiritual authority and power. This was the inheritance the enemy had successfully stolen from Adam and Eve in the garden by convincing them that they could be gods without God. It was the inheritance he then tried unsuccessfully to steal from the Last Adam in the desert by showing him the kingdoms of the earth and saying, "I will give you all their authority and splendor; it has been given to me, and I can give it to anyone I want to. If you worship me, it will all be yours" (Luke 4:6-7). When that temptation failed, the enemy turned to other resources to oppose Jesus' threat to his authority—humans he had deceived into thinking that *they* had spiritual authority. Jesus alone saw clearly what was hiding behind the religious leaders' self-righteousness—"You belong to your father, the devil, and you want to carry out your father's desires" (John 8:44).

The second parable—the parable of the prodigal son—also shines a spotlight on the deception of the religious leaders around their spiritual authority, and how it caused them to not only miss but oppose His mission as the Messiah. To a mixed audience of two groups—"tax collectors and sinners" and "Pharisees and teachers of the law" (Luke 15:1-2)—Jesus told this story about two sons. Both sons wanted their inheritance from their father but went about trying to get it in different ways. The younger son basically told the father, "I wish you were dead now," demanded his inheritance, left the country, and squandered it. The elder worked quietly away on the father's estate, silently saying, "I'll keep a low profile and wait for you to die so I can inherit." Eventually, the younger son repented and decided to come home to the father. When the elder son heard that the father had reinstated his younger brother and was celebrating his return, he showed his true colors. The mask of the good, faithful son fell away to reveal an angry son who was bitterly offended that his father would forgive his rebellious younger brother and give him access to the family and inheritance. He insulted the father to his face for showing mercy and all but admitted that everything he did for the father was motivated by what he was supposed to get as the "righteous" son.

Jesus' message was bold but clear. Sinners and Pharisees are both sons of the Father with the same problem. They are both disconnected from the Father and driven by the goal of self-preservation. They are both using the Father to get what they want from Him, and both, in their heart of hearts, want Him *dead* and out of the way so they can do what they want. Because they have the same problem, they need the same solution: repentance and reconciliation with the Father. The example of the younger brother in the story is Jesus' promise that when they choose this solution, they will find no punishment in the Father's heart—only His joy in forgiving and restoring relationship with them. But Jesus ends this parable on a cliffhanger that essentially asks the Pharisees, "Your problem is that you don't have a problem . . . but you do. So what will you do? Will you admit that you're just as disconnected and self-interested as these tax collectors and sinners, and change your goal to connection with the Father? Will you repent too?"

Of course, as the story plays out, it is not the repentant sinners but the unrepentant, self-righteous, judgmental, punishing religious leaders who ended up executing Jesus. They would not surrender their punishment paradigm. They would not allow the Son to step into the matrix of their power and start changing the rules—offering forgiveness and reconciliation not only to sinners but also to them, thereby exposing that they are not morally superior judges who have the authority to play God but who need to repent and receive mercy, and ultimately doing away with their right to judge and punish. They rightly recognized that the coming of His kingdom, the kingdom of repentance, forgiveness, and reconciliation between God and man, meant the end of their rule and reign. They punished and killed Jesus as a last-ditch effort—masterminded and empowered by the enemy who had deceived them—to force Him to submit to their false spiritual authority and stolen kingdom.

In fact, the crucifixion of Jesus was the climax of the rebellion that began in the garden, the most extreme attempt we humans could make, as deceived puppets of the enemy, to finally overthrow God and establish our own kingdom of darkness on the earth apart from Him. It was the grand statement of the punishment paradigm—the destructive unleashing of all our fear of punishment in the ultimate act of self-preservation to disconnect ourselves finally from God. Remember, our addiction to punishment is the expression of our addiction to being our own gods, which is the bondage of sin. Punishment is the false power of the enemy we exercise as slaves of his kingdom. There could be no greater move we could make with this power than to punish God Himself.

But again, none of this caught Jesus by surprise. In fact, He came to earth to bring our rebellion to a head, as if to say, "You want to be your own gods? You want me dead? Well, I'll come to you in the flesh so you can finally follow through on that. Take out all your anger, bitterness, offense, judgment, pain, and fear on me. Kill me." What Jesus' punishers couldn't see, however, was that by "taking our punishment" (which not only means "being punished on our behalf," but also "allowing us to punish Him"), He would undermine everything about how the punishment paradigm worked. Jesus was neither a shame-filled victim nor an angry avenger. He had absolutely no fear of punishment in Him. He was not trying to control or manipulate anyone. And His goal was obviously not self-preservation, for He committed the ultimate act of self-sacrifice to remove our sin and pursue the goal of reconnection with us.

NO SEPARATION

Jesus' beliefs, motives, behavior, and goal countered the punishment paradigm in every aspect, because He, the Father, and the Spirit do not operate from this paradigm. Once we understand this, the idea that the Father punished His Son on the cross becomes absurd. Though "*we* considered [Jesus] punished by God" (Isaiah 53:4), in reality, Father, Son, and Spirit were working together to absorb both our sin and its punishment and bear them away from us. And they could do this because the paradigm they operate from—the paradigm of love—is stronger than sin and punishment.

Many people interpret Jesus' quoting Psalm 22 on the cross—"My God, my God, why have You forsaken me?"—as the Father turning His face and abandoning His Son to suffering and death. They believe Jesus allowed our sin to separate Him from the Father as it separated us. But sin doesn't separate us from God in the way we typically think. When we sin, God doesn't turn His face from us, but in the deception of sin, we imagine that He does. This imagined rejection and punishment produces the fear of punishment, which leads us to run and hide from God like Adam and Eve did in the garden. Separation from God is the false reality we end up living in by believing the enemy's lies and accusations about Him and ourselves.

On the cross, Jesus allowed Himself to enter our sin-distorted view of the Father, to feel our terror and shame, so that He could finally expose that nightmare for what it was—an utter lie—and the truth for what it is—that nothing can separate us from the love of God. In surrendering to death, Jesus was not submitting to His Father's punishment but to ours, while trusting the Father to bring Him through the ordeal of death and back to life again. Unlike Adam and Eve in the garden, He trusted fully in the goodness of His Father to the end, and His faith was rewarded. The Father brought Him out of the grave. And through Jesus' act of sacrificial dying and the Father's act of resurrecting Him back to life, together they ratified and consummated the new covenant, while laying out the terms of this relationship and how we can enter it. We simply follow in the steps of trust laid out by Jesus, believing that He was the offering for sin and punishment once and for all, enabling God to extend free and full forgiveness and bring us back into life-giving connection with Him.

Before we look at the incredible reality of living in this new covenant, however, it's important to touch on the issue of wrath and eternal punishment—hell. Jesus came to put an end to sin and punishment, but He also talked about hell more than anyone in the Bible. Why? Because He wanted us to understand where we end up when we refuse God's many kind offers to repent and be forgiven and reconciled to Him. Like Pharaoh, and like the Israelites who died in the desert, we can choose to harden our hearts repeatedly to God, and the ultimate expression of His wrath is when He finally "gives us over" to our chosen state (Romans 1:24, 26). The only thing that can separate us from His love, in the end, is ourselves willfully choosing that separation. And when we choose that into eternity, we end up in eternal punishment—hell.

Tim Keller succinctly sums up the reality of hell, and how we end up there:

> [Hell] is simply one's freely chosen identity apart from God on a trajectory into infinity. We see this process "writ small" in addictions to drugs, alcohol, gambling, and pornography. First, there is disintegration, because as time goes on you need more and more of the addictive substance to get an equal kick, which leads to less and less satisfaction. Second, there is the isolation, as increasingly you blame others and circumstances in order to justify your behavior. "No one understands! Everyone is against me!" is muttered in greater and greater self-pity and self-absorption. When we build our lives on anything but God, that thing—though a good thing—becomes an enslaving addiction, something we *have* to have to be happy. Personal disintegration happens on a broader scale. In eternity, this disintegration goes on forever. There is increasing isolation, denial, delusion, and self-absorption. When you lose all humility you are out of touch with reality. No one ever asks to leave hell. The very idea of heaven seems to them a sham.

In his fantasy *The Great Divorce*, C. S. Lewis describes a busload of people from hell who come to the outskirts of heaven. There they are urged to leave behind the sins that have trapped them in hell—but they refuse. Lewis's descriptions of these people are striking because we recognize in them the self-delusion and self-absorption that are "writ small" in our own addictions.

> *Hell begins with a grumbling mood, always complaining, always blaming others . . . but you are still distinct from it. You may even criticize it in yourself and wish you could stop it. But there may come a day when you can no longer. Then there will be no you left to criticize the mood or even to enjoy it, but just the grumble itself, going on forever like a machine. It is not a question of God "sending us" to hell. In each of us there is something growing, which will BE Hell unless it is nipped in the bud.*

The people in hell are miserable, but Lewis shows us why. We see raging like unchecked flames their pride, their paranoia, their self-pity, their certainty that everyone else is wrong, that everyone else is an idiot! All their humility is gone, and thus so is their sanity. They are utterly, finally locked in a prison of their own self-centeredness, and their pride progressively expands into a bigger and bigger mushroom cloud. They continue to go to pieces forever, blaming everyone but themselves. Hell is that, writ large. That is why it is a travesty to picture God casting people into a pit who are crying "I'm sorry! Let me out!" The people on the bus from hell in Lewis's parable would rather have their "freedom," as they define it, than salvation. Their delusion is that, if they glorified God, they would somehow lose power and freedom, but in a supreme and tragic irony, their choice has ruined their own potential for greatness. Hell is, as Lewis says, "the greatest monument to human freedom." As Romans 1:24 says, God "gave them up to . . . their desires." All God does in the end with people is give them what they most want, including freedom from himself. What could be more fair than that? Lewis writes:

> *There are only two kinds of people—those who say "Thy will be done" to God or those to whom God in the end says, "Thy will be done." All that are in Hell choose it. Without that self-choice it wouldn't be Hell. No soul that seriously and constantly desires joy will ever miss it.*[12]

This is the sobering reality we must all reckon with—that despite all God has done to free us from slavery to sin and punishment, we could still choose to stay locked eternally in the darkness of the punishment paradigm, addicted to our victimhood, vengeance, shame, fear, control, and self-preservation. Unless we choose the path of repentance, we are choosing a lifetime of punishment over a life of no punishment in the new covenant. We are choosing hell over heaven.

THE NEW COVENANT PARADIGM

When we enter the new covenant through faith in Jesus, we become members of humanity 2.0. Our identity and nature radically change by being restored to relationship with the Father through the Son, and it is on the foundation of this new identity, and through the power of this new nature, that we begin to learn to live in the new relational paradigm of love. In the process, we see with ever-increasing clarity that our lives

---

[12] Timothy Keller, *The Reason for God* (New York, NY: Penguin Publishing Group, 2018) Kindle Edition, pp. 77-78.

in the old punishment paradigm were based on a false identity or lack of identity—we were orphans. Now we are sons and daughters who share in Christ's nature, Spirit, and access to the Father, all of which lead us to embrace an entirely different set of core beliefs, motives, behaviors, and goals:

The Punishment Paradigm	
Identity	Orphan/Slave
Core Belief	My flaws and failures make me unworthy of love, belonging, and connection. I deserve disconnection and punishment. So does everyone else with flaws and failures.
Motive	Fear of punishment/disconnection
Behavior Strategies	3. Avoid punishment—either by hiding and fitting in through 'pleasing, perfecting, and performing,' or by refusing to fit in by rebelling and making my own rules. 4. Punish others when they scare, hurt, or offend me.
Goal	Self-preservation

The New Covenant Paradigm	
Identity	Son/Daughter of God
Core Belief	Through Jesus, I have become a son or daughter who is worthy of love, belonging, and connection. My mistakes do not disqualify me from the Father's love. Instead, they are precisely where I learn the depth of His love, forgiveness, and commitment to transform me into a mature child who looks like Jesus.
Motive	Love
Behavior Strategies	Pursue connection, even when it's scary, painful, or offensive
Goal	Connection

Notice that in the new covenant paradigm, the belief that we deserve punishment, the fear of punishment, and the behavior of punishment all go away. There is no punishment in the new covenant of love. This is why John says, "There is no fear in love. But perfect love drives out fear, because fear has to do with punishment. The one who fears is not made perfect in love" (1 John 4:18). Punishment goes away, not because sin goes away (yet), but because in this new covenant, there is only one response to sin: forgiveness. This has two critical implications that must form the bedrock of our thinking as sons and daughters in this covenant.

First, we need to understand that we can and will still sin as new covenant believers. Yes, the ultimate trajectory of maturing in Christ is that we will be sinless in thought and action just like Him. But getting there involves a process of confronting and unlearning sin in our lives. We will make messes, but because we are living in a covenant of forgiveness, our experience of sin is completely different than it is when we are trapped in the punishment paradigm. Instead of being crushed by the enemy's condemnation and shame, which only pours gas on the flames of our fear of punishment and selfish, self-destructive behavior, we experience the Holy Spirit's loving conviction that we are violating our relationship with God, ourselves, and others, His reminders of the truth of who we really are, and His power to repent and be reconciled and restored. Instead of punishment for sin, we encounter only His love and forgiveness, which means that our sin actually becomes a place where the revelation of His forgiveness and love grows deeper in our lives, bringing us closer to Him and maturing us into His likeness. Of course, as Paul emphasized, this doesn't mean we should sin on purpose—it simply means that when we do sin, because we will as we grow up in Christ, we can be confident that we won't be punished, but disciplined with love into greater freedom from sin.

The other obvious implication of forgiveness being the only response to sin in the new covenant is that we must always forgive others—something we should do better and better as we receive His forgiveness for ourselves amid our sinful messes. It is humbling and awesome to think that Christ has actually given us His authority to forgive sins: "If you forgive anyone's sins, their sins are forgiven; if you do not forgive them, they are not forgiven" (John 20:23). It is equally sobering to understand that if we do not forgive others, we are stepping out from the covering of the new covenant, forfeiting our own forgiveness and coming back under condemnation, and aligning ourselves with the punishment paradigm and the enemy who empowers it.

Jesus emphasized the seriousness of not forgiving in His parable about the servant who was forgiven a great debt:

> Therefore, the kingdom of heaven is like a king who wanted to settle accounts with his servants. As he began the settlement, a man who owed him ten thousand bags of gold was brought to him. Since he was not able to pay, the master ordered that he and his wife and his children and all that he had be sold to repay the debt. At this the servant fell on his knees before him. "Be patient with me," he begged, "and I will pay back everything." The servant's master took pity on him, canceled the debt and let him go. But when that servant went out, he found one of his fellow servants who owed him a hundred silver coins. He grabbed him and began to choke him. "Pay back what you owe me!" he demanded. His fellow servant fell to his knees and begged him, "Be patient with me, and I will pay it back." But he refused. Instead, he went off and had the man thrown into prison until he could pay the debt. When the other servants saw what had happened, they were outraged and went and told their master everything that had happened. Then the master called the servant in. "You wicked servant," he said, "I canceled all that debt of yours because you begged me to. Shouldn't you have had mercy

> on your fellow servant just as I had on you?" In anger his master handed him over to the jailers to be tortured, until he should pay back all he owed. This is how my heavenly Father will treat each of you unless you forgive your brother or sister from your heart. (Matthew 18:21-35)

Clearly, the Father does not mess around with this issue of forgiveness in our lives. Our debt to Him could only be paid through the horror of the cross and the grave, and He gladly endured that to offer us forgiveness. Refusing forgiveness to others for their offenses against us demonstrates a callous heart that is completely unimpressed by God's sacrificial love, and God deals with such hardness of heart by "handing us over" to the prison of punishment. Again, punishment is where we end up when we refuse to participate in His covenant of forgiveness.

WALKING IT OUT

Our transformation from orphans to mature sons and daughters is the journey of a lifetime, and receiving and giving forgiveness are essential, ongoing practices on that journey. Guess what? That means that life in the new covenant is messy. We are all in a process of allowing God to dismantle the lies, fear, and selfishness of the punishment paradigm in our hearts and form new hearts of flesh that can love like He loves. We are all learning to let love drive out fear and retrain us to choose connection over self-preservation *every time*. We are all discovering what it means to repent, reconcile, and be restored in our relationships with God, ourselves, and others.

The beauty of life in the new covenant, however, is that our transformation is happening not in spite of our messes, but through them. By removing the fear of punishment, the Father has opened a way for us to lean into our sin, mistakes, pain, and brokenness with Him and experience the victory of the cross in our own stories, relationships, families, churches, and communities.

In the second half of this book, we're going to look at how we practically work through our messes in the new covenant. We're going to cover the classic questions that most of us struggle with as we are trying to grow in relating to God, ourselves, and others in a punishment-free way:

- How do we confront others effectively?
- What is repentance? How do we walk it out? How do you know when someone has repented?
- What is reconciliation? What are the steps to reconcile a broken relationship?
- What is restoration? How do you know when a person or relationship is restored?

In answering these questions, I'm going to share the best of the practical insights and wisdom I've learned over many years walking with people who are in a mess, as well as stories that illustrate both what to do and what not to do. In the process, I want to equip you with peace, faith, and hope to advance in your own journey of maturity and become consistent in living out and cultivating this punishment-free new covenant culture.

CHAPTER 6

DISCIPLINE IN THE NEW COVENANT

One Friday night when my son Taylor was sixteen, he didn't come home. His curfew was midnight. At 1 a.m., I texted him asking when he would be home. No answer. At 3 a.m., I texted, "Are you on your way, or should I call the cops?" Nothing.

When I got up in the morning just before seven, I asked Sheri, "Is Taylor in his bed?"

"No," she confirmed.

"He didn't come home last night."

Immediately, Sheri began calling every single parent of Taylor's friends to try and find out where he might be—just the sort of call every parent loves to wake up to on a Saturday morning.

An hour later, Taylor walked in the front door. I met him with an outstretched hand and calmly said two words. "Keys. Phone."

As he handed them over, Taylor launched into excuses. "I fell asleep at Jake's house. I didn't have a charger, and neither does Jake. There was no way for me to call."

I remained wordless, looking at him, until he gave up and headed for his bedroom. Five hours later, at one in the afternoon, Taylor reemerged in his underwear, looking like a refugee from a prison camp. Apparently after "sleeping all night at Jake's," he'd still been exhausted. I took one look at his face and thought, *That is not the kid I want to talk to. That kid doesn't have a problem. That kid is nowhere near repenting for anything. That kid is a victim.* I remained silent, and after a while, he returned to his room.

At 3 p.m., one of Taylor's friends called our landline. Seconds after Taylor picked up the phone, I watched the refugee transform back into an animated teenager. "Oh, dude, I forgot that was today! All right, okay." Apparently, his friend had reminded him that they had a big videogame tournament planned for that night—they had even bought matching shirts for it. The tournament was supposed to begin at 7 p.m., so Taylor had four hours to try to turn his situation around. Fifteen minutes later, he had showered, dressed, and returned to the living room with his most charming smile pointed at Sheri and me.

Now that's the kid I want to talk to right there, I thought. *He wants something. He has hope.*

"Hey, Dad," Taylor said. "I was just wondering if we could talk."

This was what I had been praying for. I led him out to the back patio and asked quietly, "What did you want to talk about?"

"Oh, I just wanted to say I'm sorry for not coming home last night."

"Okay. Why does that matter?"

Taylor looked stumped. "I don't know. I just thought . . . I mean, you want me to come home at night. I was supposed to come home."

"Well, what are you sorry about?"

"I'm . . . sorry that I didn't come home?" He looked confused.

"Tay, I guess I just don't understand what you're apologizing for." My tone was calm, quiet, and curious.

"I'm apologizing because I didn't come home. And I was supposed to."

"Why does that matter?"

"I don't know. I just thought it did."

"Well, I'm really not sure what you're apologizing for."

Taylor groaned with frustration. "Ugh! Why are you making this so hard?"

"You were the one who wanted to apologize. I'm just wondering what you're apologizing for. You can't even tell me why, so I'm not sure what we're doing out here."

At this point, our conversation was interrupted by a phone call from my lawyer. "I have to take this call," I told Taylor, "but I'll come back."

When we finally reconvened, it was 5 p.m., and Taylor was starting to look a little desperate. "Okay, Dad, I'm sorry," he began. "You guys were probably worried and didn't know if I was dead or alive or anything. And that was causing a lot of stress. I'm sorry for that."

"Why does it matter if we're up all night worried about where you are?" I pressed. "Why does that matter?"

"I feel like I'm somebody in your office and you're just asking him all the questions!" He burst out.

"Taylor, I don't understand why you don't understand what the problem is."

"I don't know what the problem is! I don't know what to say!"

"Do you want some help with that?"

Taylor paused. "Yeah."

"Okay, well, Taylor, I'll just tell you how I experienced you," I began, looking directly at him, my tone still low and gentle. "I feel so disrespected and so reduced in the value of your life. It's so hurtful. I feel like when you sort through the priorities of things that you're going to take care of, I'm down there around twenty. And I don't know how that happened. I don't know how Mom and I fell to twenty on your priority list. But last night was an example of that. It seems like you're going to take care of twenty things before you take care of me and Mom."

"You feel like that?" Taylor asked, eyes wide.

"Yeah, I feel like that. Last night was just a glaring example of the value and priority of our relationship to you."

He shook his head. "Well, that's not true. You and Mom are the most important people in my life."

"Last night was not an example of that," I repeated.

"Well, I'm sorry about that," he said sincerely. "I'm sorry for being disrespectful. And that will never happen again."

I looked at him with a hopeful smile. "That's really all I need to hear. Did you want your phone and your keys?"

An hour later, Taylor took off for his videogame tournament. And he never stayed out all night again.

PUNISHMENT VS. DISCIPLINE

What happened in this story? First, I'll point out what *didn't* happen: punishment. I didn't take Taylor's keys and phone to pay him back for scaring and hurting Sheri and me. I did it to create leverage by introducing a consequence for his poor choice. I wanted to remind him of the value and importance of his relationship with us, so I attracted his attention by hanging on to something he cared about—which happened to be direct benefits of having us as parents—until he was willing to push through the tension and pain, find the problem, take personal responsibility for it, and ask for forgiveness. My goal all along was to forgive him, but I knew he wouldn't be able to receive it until he got in touch with what needed to be forgiven. In the end, his choice to walk through the consequence and discover what was really at stake—protecting our connection—reinforced the value of our connection in his heart. When future opportunities to violate connection arose, he had both a new understanding of the value of our connection and a new motivation to protect it that made those opportunities unappealing.

What happened in this story was *discipline*. Though "discipline" and "punishment" are often used interchangeably, biblically, they are completely different experiences that produce very different results. As we saw in Chapter 1, Ben Armstrong noted the stark difference in his own case: ". . . when the first affair happened, I was punished . . . The second time, I was disciplined." Punishment set him up to fail again, but discipline empowered him to learn from and overcome his failure.

Discipline comes from the same word as disciple, which means "learner." But what exactly are we learning? The famous passage on discipline in Hebrews 12 shows us what, how, and why we learn:

> . . . we must let go of every wound that has pierced us and the sin we so easily fall into. Then we will be able to run life's marathon race with passion and determination, for the path has been already marked out before us . . . [Consider] carefully how Jesus faced such intense opposition from sinners who opposed their own souls, so that you won't become worn down and cave in under life's pressures. After all, you have not yet reached the point of sweating blood in your opposition to sin. And have you forgotten his encouraging words spoken to you as his children? He said,

> "My child, don't underestimate the value
> of the discipline and training of the Lord God,
> or get depressed when he has to correct you.
> For the Lord's training of your life
> is the evidence of his faithful love.
> And when he draws you to himself,
> it proves you are his delightful child."
>
> Fully embrace God's correction as part of your training, for he is doing what any loving father does for his children. For who has ever heard of a child who never had to be corrected? We all should welcome God's discipline as the validation of authentic sonship. For if we have never once endured his correction it only proves we are strangers and not sons . . .
>
> Now all discipline seems to be more pain than pleasure at the time, yet later it will produce a transformation of character, bringing a harvest of righteousness and peace to those who yield to it. (Hebrews 12:1, 3-8, 11 TPT)

The first thing to notice here is that in the new covenant, discipline is a relational exchange between the Father and His children. Though in the body of Christ we do experience discipline through human authority figures like parents and leaders, that discipline is only functioning correctly when those figures accurately represent the heart of the Father and lead and equip people to connect more deeply with Him. Every discipline scenario is first and foremost about this relationship.

The second thing to see is the Father's goal in this exchange. He wants to heal us of our wounds, train us to overcome sin, and transform our character so that we become mature sons and daughters who look like Jesus. In other words, in the new covenant, discipline is focused on benefitting the person who has made the mess. In the punishment paradigm, the focus is on protecting the interests of everyone but the offender, but in the new covenant, we understand that helping the mess-maker clean up their mess is ultimately what will produce justice and healing for everyone affected by it. Instead of taking the mess away or requiring the mess-maker to deal with the consequences alone, the Father's heart is to walk through the consequences alongside them, bringing comfort, correction, wisdom, and courage as they clean it up. This is His process for helping His kids unlearn the punishment paradigm and rebuild their lives in His punishment-free relational paradigm of love, trust, and freedom. Where else can He best show us that His heart is not to punish us, but to remove our shame, forgive us, free us from the fear of punishment, and lead us into loving, safe connection with Him than in our messes and mistakes? Where else can we best grow and learn than by seeing our Father redeem our failures and use them to make us wise?

Now, Hebrews doesn't shy away from the reality that walking through the consequences of our mess with the Father is painful. In fact, pain is the element punishment and discipline hold in common. The difference is that with punishment, our experience with pain only increases our fear of punishment and encourages us to harden our hearts even more. But with discipline, pain breaks our hearts and softens them. To put it another way, the pain we experience in a punishment process is the pain of fear, shame, anxiety, intimidation, and disconnection, and typically we react to this pain in ways that end up doubling down on the behaviors that caused it in the first place. In the discipline process, our pain comes from the awareness that we have violated our connections with God, ourselves, and others. It is the pain of grief—what Paul calls "godly sorrow"—that leads to repentance and change, through which we learn how to prevent causing more pain in the future. This is the "harvest of righteousness and peace" that only comes through the Father's discipline in our lives.

Here's a basic breakdown of the primary differences between punishment and discipline:

Punishment	**Discipline**
Upholding the rules	Restoring the relationship
Pain is inflicted/imposed	Pain is embraced
Worldly sorrow	Godly sorrow
Repentance is irrelevant	Repentance is essential
Forgiveness is irrelevant	Forgiveness is essential
Requires submission of control	Requires responsibility, self-control
Stopping bad behavior	Transforming heart
Good behavior is compliance and manipulative	Good behavior is fruit of love
Powerless	Powerful
Fear-driven	Love-driven
Goal of self-preservation	Goal of connection
External law	Internal law

THREE DIMENSIONS OF SPIRITUAL MATURITY

Though this book is written for everyone, one of my greatest hopes is that it would help to equip leaders, especially in the home and the church, to represent the Father's heart toward people making sinful messes. Leaders are responsible to create and protect culture. It's not a stretch to say that immature leadership is the primary reason so many people in the body of Christ have encountered either punishment or a lack of healthy discipline when they've made a mess. We desperately need leaders who are trained and seasoned in the practice of punishment-free confrontation and discipline to establish a culture where mess-makers are invited into and led through the journey of repentance, reconciliation, and restoration.

In Galatians, Paul says: "Brethren, if a man is overtaken in any trespass, you who are spiritual restore such a one in a spirit of gentleness, considering yourself lest you also be tempted" (Galatians 6:1 NKJV). In the next chapter, we'll look at how to confront someone "in a spirit of gentleness" and lead them on the path to restoration. But first I want to clarify who Paul is talking to when he says, "you who are spiritual." He means "you who are spiritually mature." In my experience and observation, there are three dimensions of spiritual maturity we need in order to offer help to those "overtaken in a trespass": humble self-awareness, loving discernment, and relational wisdom.

When Paul says to "consider yourself lest you also be tempted," he is instructing us to practice humble self-awareness. The word "consider" comes from the same word from which we get "skeptical." Many of us have this misguided idea that the spiritually mature are those who no longer struggle with sin in their own lives. The biblical picture, however, is that the spiritually mature are those who have become disillusioned—in a good way—about their areas of weakness by walking their own journey of discipline with the Father. They live with a healthy self-doubt because they know from experience that they can easily end up in a situation that will test them in a way they've never been tested and reveal weakness they never knew was there. This self-doubt and disillusionment is healthy, however, because it does not lead to shame, but to healing, growth, and increased trust and dependence on the Father. The reason Paul cheerfully calls himself the chief of sinners (see 1 Timothy 1:15) is not some morbid self-punishment, but the humble joy of a son who can say, "I'm not free of all weakness, but I am free of fear and shame about my weakness. Therefore, I live with freedom, watching myself so I don't fall, but also confident that my Father will correct and restore me if I do."

Humble self-awareness gives birth to loving discernment in our lives. The "loving" part is essential. Many people mistakenly think that the "gift of discernment" is for figuring out what's wrong with other people and using that to justify criticizing or creating distance from them—that is, punishing—those they have judged offensive. This is exactly what Jesus told us *not to do* in the Sermon on the Mount:

> "Refuse to be a critic full of bias toward others, and judgment will not be passed on you. For you'll be judged by the same standard that you've used to judge others. The measurement you use on them will be used on you. Why would you focus on the flaw in someone else's life and yet fail to notice the glaring flaws of your own? How could you say to your friend, 'Let me show you where you're wrong,' when you're guilty of even more? You're being hypercritical and a hypocrite! First acknowledge your own 'blind spots' and deal with them, and then you'll be capable of dealing with the 'blind spot' of your friend." (Matthew 7:1-5 TPT)

The word "discern" means to judge the difference between two things. It does *not* mean to judge someone guilty and worthy of punishment. When we do this, we demonstrate that we are not operating from a new covenant paradigm, but from the punishment paradigm. We are wielding the gift of discernment with the wrong spirit. This is what Jesus confronted His disciples about in Luke 9. When a Samaritan village refused entry to Jesus and His disciples, James and John asked, "Lord, do You want us to command fire to come down from heaven and consume them, just as Elijah did?" Jesus said, 'You do not know what manner of spirit you are of. For the Son of Man did not come to destroy men's lives but to save [them]'" (Luke 9:54-56 NKJV). James and John looked at the Samaritans rejecting them and saw sinners worthy of destruction. Jesus saw those worthy of saving. The reason they looked at the same people and the same behavior but discerned them in completely different ways was the result of the "spirit" they were operating from.

There are basically two spirits we can be "of." In Romans 8, Paul describes them as the spirit of slavery to fear and the spirit of adoption: "The Spirit you received does not make you slaves, so that you live in fear again; rather, the Spirit you received brought about your adoption to sonship. And by him we cry, "Abba, Father" (Romans 8:15). Similarly, in his letter to Timothy, he says, "For the Spirit God gave us does not make us timid, but gives us power, love and self-discipline" (2 Timothy 1:7).

We are either operating from the fear of punishment that keeps us disconnected from the Father and enslaved to our old, orphan identity and the punishment paradigm (Paul calls it the "flesh"), or we are operating from loving connection with the Father as sons and daughters led by the Spirit. Spiritual growth is all about allowing the Holy Spirit to expose and cast out the fear of punishment wherever it shows up in our lives with His perfect (mature) love (see 1 John 4:18). This practice of distinguishing fear and love, first in our own hearts and then in others, is how we become "the mature, who because of practice have [our] senses trained to discern good and evil" (Hebrews 5:14 NASB). Realigning our hearts from fear to love removes our "blind spots" so we can see ourselves and others from the Father's perspective. The ultimate litmus test for spiritual maturity and loving discernment, Jesus said, is whether we can point the Father's love toward our enemies: "I tell you, love your enemies and pray for those who persecute you, that you may be children of your Father in heaven . . . Be perfect [mature], therefore, as your heavenly Father is perfect" (Matthew 5:44, 48). When we look at our enemies, do we see what Jesus sees? Do we see scary, messy sinners who deserve hatred and punishment, or do we see sons and daughters for whom the Father sacrificed everything to love and restore? Only when we see the latter can we be trusted to sit down with someone in a mess and discern correctly what the problem is and how to help them solve it.

Lastly, spiritual maturity involves relational wisdom. Wisdom is the ability to apply knowledge and understanding skillfully according to the situation. Relational wisdom is where we take the lessons we have learned through our own journey of growth in self-awareness and loving discernment and put them to work to help someone else. Here are four specific areas of knowledge and understanding that are either critical, or at least very helpful, for being able to lead someone through new covenant discipline.

First, you should learn as much as you can about God's design and purpose for people, and His vision for human flourishing. It's easy and tempting to focus on our flaws and how we fall short of the glory of God without first anchoring ourselves in the truth that God's purposes and power are greater. He created us in His image for life-giving, loving connection with Him, ourselves, and one another. This is the context in which we were designed to have our core needs met and to thrive, and He is fully committed to fulfilling that ultimate purpose in our lives.

Second, you should learn about sin and how it violates our design and purpose. Genesis 3 lays out the basic origin and development of sin in our hearts. It begins with mistrusting God, leads to putting ourselves on the throne (idolatry), and results in bondage to shame and the fear of punishment. Every sinful behavior in our lives is rooted in this pattern.

Third, you should learn about the gospel—God's solution for sin—and how it works in our lives through the journey of discipleship. In this generation, we must combat many misconceptions about the gospel. It is not about getting "saved" so we go to heaven when we die. It is about entering a reconciled relationship with the Father, ourselves, and others and receiving His Holy Spirit so we can grow up in those relationships. This is where God undoes sin in our lives by leading us from mistrust to trust, from idolatry to true worship, and from fear to love.

Lastly, it can be very helpful to invest in some training in counseling and coaching disciplines. The Bible and other spiritual writings have much to offer in this area, specifically in the areas of inner healing and deliverance. I have also found plenty of helpful knowledge and tools in areas of modern psychology, such as emotional intelligence, and personality and behavior typologies such as Myers-Briggs, DISC, StrengthsFinder, and the Enneagram. Beyond the insights these tools provide, they also provide language that can broaden our ability to communicate effectively with more people. If people are familiar with the language of a certain concept or tool, it provides a kind of shorthand for discussing the behavior and problem behind it. For example, I've been investing in learning more about the Enneagram lately because I've been finding that more and more people are familiar with it. In a moment, I'll show you how I apply insights from the DISC behavior style framework in helping someone who is dealing with a mess.

There's one more key ingredient that is absolutely critical for applying these areas of knowledge and understanding with relational wisdom. We must always be leaning into the voice and power of the Holy Spirit. One of the clearest expressions of spiritual maturity is that we trust Him to lead and provide what is needed in the discipline process instead of relying on our own knowledge and wisdom apart from Him. He is the true Helper who knows exactly what's going on in the heart of the person in front of us and what solution they need. He is the Spirit of Truth who will lead them into all truth. He is the one who will guide us in using His gifts of healing, prophecy, discernment, and deliverance to help people get free. Ultimately, He is the one who will discipline this son or daughter as they need to be disciplined. Our job is trust and follow Him.

APPROACHING DISCIPLINE WITH SPIRITUAL MATURITY

Leaning into the Holy Spirit is where I start in a conversation that involves confrontation or someone needing my help. I begin an internal dialogue that sounds something like, "Lord, please help me find what You are doing in this situation with this person." I know that my experience, training, and discernment are going to kick in quite quickly and naturally. In fact, I have an entire model, which I will introduce in the next chapter, for punishment-free confrontation that leads people to repentance, reconciliation, and restoration. I also know none of that will help, and can even get in the way, if I don't find out how God wants to bring heaven to earth in this person's life. My primary goal is not to encounter this person with my knowledge, tools, and wisdom, but to lead them into an encounter with a loving Father. And while I don't know how that encounter will unfold, I also carry hope and faith that it will happen, because I've seen it happen over and over again—both in my own life and in the lives of those I have helped.

Along with this posture of leaning and expectancy, I do bring a basic framework of understanding that orients me to ask certain questions, observe behavior, and sort the information I'm receiving efficiently so I can start to zero in on the problem that needs to be solved. I know that people are far more predictable than they care to admit, and there are really only a few ways people go wrong. The deepest, core issue is usually that they've experienced damage in their ability or willingness to trust themselves, others, and God. One of the questions that often proves fruitful for helping someone find their problem is, "Why are you so afraid to trust God?" Beyond this, I typically find that what they are struggling to trust God about is connected to one of their core needs. The behavioral mess they have created is based in their flawed attempt to meet this need on their own through illegitimate or unhealthy means, which has produced painful consequences and fueled shame and fear of punishment in their lives.

As humans, we all have similar psychological and social needs, but our personalities and behavior styles organize them in different orders of priority. The DISC behavior style profile is a tool I have found helpful in discerning the core needs people are trying to meet on their own. It assesses human behavior in four areas—our approach to challenges and problems (D-Dominant), our approach to ideas and influence

(I-Influencer), our approach to the pace of life and change (S-Steadfast), and our approach to rules and best practices (C-Conscientious). One of the insights my DISC training has provided me with is an understanding of the core needs that drive each behavior style. Here's a basic breakdown of the needs of each style:

- **Dominant** needs significance, power, success, predictability, and control
- **Influencer** needs freedom, fun, expression, approval, and adventure
- **Steadfast** needs connection, to serve, family, and to belong
- **Conscientious** needs security, accuracy, information, and truth

When people in each of these styles are not trusting God to meet these needs in healthy ways, they struggle with fear that those needs will not be met, which leads them to act out in different ways to protect themselves:

	Motivational Needs	Internal Struggle	Expressions of Powerlessness
D	Significance	Insecurity	Anger
I	Freedom	Rejection	Optimism/Trust
S	Connection	Conflict	Unemotional
C	Security	Failure	Fear

Here are some examples of how I weave this tool in with discernment and leaning into the Holy Spirit.

I know a couple who are both high **D**s. They've been married over twenty-five years and repeatedly clash over certain issues in the same pattern. It starts when she does something he doesn't like, and he withdraws until she confronts him on it. He denies that he is withdrawing and they end up in a verbal conflict that leaves them both hurt and scared of each other. Eventually the tension dies down, and they resume some normalcy until the next conflict ramps up.

When the husband comes to me asking for help in addressing this broken dynamic, my knowledge that he and his wife are both high **D**s tells me they must both win in any conflict. They both long for respect and value (significance), and because they are not getting what they need, they feel powerless. This evokes a deep threat of being exploited, misunderstood, or replaced in relationship. The trigger of powerlessness leads both players in this marriage to toxic anger levels. This is how they both end up hurt, scared, and disconnected in the relationship.

If I help this man focus on what he is angry about—the injustice or behavior of his wife he so disapproves of—then he just builds his case and becomes lost in his emotion of anger. But, if we pivot and go after the real issue he's dealing with—powerlessness—he now sees something he's not seen before. He sees that he is trying to control his wife because he feels out of control. She's doing the same thing. When he realizes that he is trying to control her with the silent treatment, accusations, blame, and hostility, he sees what he is contributing to the problem. Repentance for him is to recognize when he feels powerless, which is usually hiding under his anger, and to either verbalize that or to devise a plan to control himself. He never wants to hurt or scare his wife but has resorted to that for twenty-five years because he thought he couldn't control his anger. It's not his anger he needs to control—it is his love.

Here are some questions I often end up asking someone with a **D** behavior style:

- You sound angry, but are you feeling more threatened, hurt, or powerless?
- What are you so afraid of?
- Did what that person did feel disrespectful to you?
- If someone is disrespectful, what do you think that means about you?
- Is it true that you are not worthy of value in a relationship?
- Who are you going to let control your anger?
- What can you do if you feel hurt?
- What can you do if you feel scared or threatened?
- What can you control if you feel powerless about what someone else is doing?
- Who controls you?
- Who protects you?
- Do you trust God in this situation?

A high-**I** woman I know is famous for her outgoing, fun-loving personality. She's immensely talented and, with her great smile and contagious laugh, quickly wins favor with absolute strangers. She seems to be the focal point of every room she enters and is one of those people who everyone wants to know. But behind the flow of her free-spiritedness is a deep need to keep affirmation and acceptance coming her way. She feels like a slave because others control what she needs: freedom and approval. She is trying to be all things to everybody but ends up being nobody to anybody.

As this woman describes to me her feelings of depression, anxiety, and being on the verge of burnout, I know that she is running from her broken spot of rejection. She is willing to lie to get acceptance and avoid a conflict. Ironically, she is courting rejection in her closest relationships because she is not careful with them. She is moody, over-sensitive, and expects her friends and team members to adjust to her needs. People are afraid to get too close because she will either explode when they don't meet her expectations, or she will disregard what they need because she is consumed with her own needs.

Some of the questions I'm going to ask her are:

- What are you so afraid of?
- What if that does happen?
- What does it mean about you if that happens?
- Whose acceptance do you need most?
- What are you willing to do to have that acceptance?
- What would happen if you told that person "no"?
- What would it take for you to face your fear of rejection?
- Do you think people believe you when you say you are sorry?
- Are you having a difficult time building trust with those closest to you?

A guy I've worked with in the past is a high **S**. He is one of the kindest people you'll ever meet. He's willing to work late and come in early. He is deeply wise, caring, and patient. There seems to be no end to his willingness to serve and please others. Social harmony is his happy place, and he constantly works his group or relational environment to make sure everyone is feeling some level of connection and sense of belonging.

However, at one point he came to me absolutely miserable because he was feeling like an unappreciated doormat in several of his relationships. He had tried to convince these people that he was an easy friend and wanted nothing more than to simply get along with them. They had simply continued to dish out abusive treatment and invalidation, and he had responded by hiding his pain and acting as though it wasn't happening. Though he was feeling dead on the inside, he continued smiling or laughing because his worst nightmare was that someone sees him as a burden or some kind of "bad guy." He was in a cycle where he had no idea how to garner or create mutually respectful relationships.

Here are some of the questions I asked him after he finished his story:

- How long does it take you to realize that you feel hurt or invalidated?
- Are you valuable enough to protect?
- What are you so afraid of?
- What does it mean about you if you get disconnected from someone that you care about?
- What is more important to you: value or a lack of conflict?
- Do you value you?

One of the high-**C** people I know is a brilliant, capable accountant. She is a perfectionist who needs to get things right . . . and to *be* right. She has a certain self-righteousness about her that she doesn't think anyone sees. She even thinks she can manipulate God into doing what she wants because she is so good at keeping what she believes are His rules.

When she comes to me and describes her struggles, it quickly becomes clear that nobody can fulfill her expectations of a relationship—including God. She is disappointed in God. Her life has numerous tragedies in it, which doesn't make sense to her. She has earned a smooth life. But because she has these rough spots, it must mean that He sees her imperfection and failings and is punishing her. She has messed up the most important thing in her life, pleasing God, and therefore deserves punishment instead of joy.

Here are some of the questions I will ask her:

- What makes you righteous: Your work or Jesus' work?
- What are you so afraid of?
- If you fail, what is true about you in that failure?
- Do you know what you need to feel in this relationship or situation?
- What about confrontation feels wrong to you?
- Can you see the truth that is missing from your perspective?
- How would you get that truth in this relationship?

Again, DISC is just one tool I have found useful for helping me understand and discern the deeper beliefs, needs, and motives behind people's behavior, especially when they are being triggered by fear. There are many other tools that you may find helpful for yourself and others. As we will see in the coming chapters, getting to these beliefs, needs, and motives is critical for helping people take the path of repentance. The whole purpose and approach of the Father's discipline in our lives is to transform us from the inside out.

SECTION III

TAKING THE UNPUNISHABLE JOURNEY

CHAPTER 7

THE FIVE Es CONFRONTATION MODEL

Over the last couple of decades, I have frequently been called on to help with a "hot mess." Classically, hot messes involve someone introducing destruction into their life at a new and unmanageable level. On a large scale, this destruction is typically caused by some immoral practice that represents a devastating betrayal—adultery, sexual immorality, theft, etc. On a smaller scale, it is caused by high levels of disrespect, dishonesty, and dishonor. In every case, however, the person's behavior has caused significant damage to their most intimate connections, and the blast radius often extends out to circles of innocent people.

It's important to mention that these are *moral messes* I step in to on the basis of relationship and authority. If someone has made a legal mess—committed murder, molested a child, driven while intoxicated—there's not a whole lot I can do. Legal authorities are the ones with the jurisdiction to determine consequences and how things will proceed. But a church leader who commits adultery, a business leader who is violating the culture of their organization, or parents who are struggling with a rebellious teenager—these are moral messes that fall under the moral authority of church leaders, business leaders, and parents. These are the kinds of messes I deal with.

Usually by the time I get called in to help with a hot mess, the person has blown through a series of unsuccessful confrontations and has been maneuvering to hide, deceive, and keep distance from others for a while. People ask me, "When should I confront an issue in a relationship?" Confrontation should happen whenever an unacceptable level of anxiety has entered the relationship—usually through some kind of disrespect or irresponsibility—and it's damaging the connection. That's the point where something will change in the relationship—either because you have a successful conversation and adjust to restore respect and responsibility and repair the connection, or because you avoid or fumble the confrontation, and choose distance to protect yourselves from each other. The reason someone ends up in a hot mess is that they have done the latter over and over. They are operating fully as an orphan in self-preservation mode, driven by shame and the fear of punishment and punishing themselves and others through distance and disconnection.

The whole purpose of new covenant confrontation is to call people out of this orphan lifestyle in the punishment paradigm and back to sonship in the new covenant. In Matthew 18, Jesus instructs us to counteract someone's downward spiral of distance and destruction by involving increasing levels of accountability and spiritual authority when we confront them. The goal of these confrontations is not to expose or excommunicate the person, but to "win them over" (see Matthew 18:15). Galatians 6:1-3 says something similar:

> My beloved friends, if you see a believer who is overtaken with a fault, may the one who overflows with the Spirit seek to restore him. *Win him over* with gentle words, which will open his heart to you and will keep you from exalting yourself over him. Love empowers us to fulfill the law of the Anointed One as we car-

> ry each other's troubles. If you think you are too important to stoop down to help another, you are living in deception. (TPT, emphasis added)

The New King James says to restore them "in a spirit of gentleness." One illustration I use to describe the spirit of gentleness is to imagine trying to pet a deer. The only way I am going to be successful is if I can convince that deer that I pose zero threat to it. That means I need to eliminate as much anxiety from the encounter as possible. I need to demonstrate that I will not attempt to control it or hurt that deer in any way. The spirit of gentleness flows from the belief, "I do not need to control you. I am not afraid of you or your mess. I am not here to punish you, shame you, or try to protect other people from you. I am just here to help you get out of this hole."

Winning people over means gaining their trust. When I confront someone, I am asking them to trust me to lead them and walk with them on a journey of repentance, reconciliation, and restoration. This is a challenge, because as I've mentioned, most of the people sitting across from me have ended up in a hot mess due to their struggle to trust God, themselves, and others. That's the reality of the orphan mindset—it is driven by mistrust. To be fair to them, however, it is rarer than it should be that people in a mess find spiritually mature believers who are actually willing to walk with them all the way through to restoration. Personally, I see it as making a covenant commitment to them, similar to the commitment I make when I agree to marry a couple. When I perform a marriage ceremony, I commit to that couple for the long haul. If they have troubles down the road, I want them to know they can call on me. The same is true of those I confront and restore. If they agree to walk with me, they can be sure that I will walk with them.

Because trust is the foundation of every successful confrontation, it is the thing I work hard to build and strengthen from the beginning of my conversation with someone. Sometimes the people in these messes are people I know well or have some significant level of relationship with. In these cases, I have a degree of trust on which to build as I interact with them. However, when I am working with people I don't know who fall under my oversight or authority, I "borrow" trust by bringing a mutual friend or trusted leader into the room. Josh and Robin Biddlecomb, the couple whose story I tell in *Culture of Honor*, were an example of this. They fell under my authority as a Bethel Church senior leader—they were students in our ministry school—but I had never met them before they showed up in my office. So, I invited two of their trusted leaders from the school to our first meeting, hoping that as Josh and Robin observed the leaders' trust in me, it would lower their anxiety. They were still pretty scared, but having trusted leaders in the room sent the message that "this is a safe place" and gave us something with which to build a connection.

At every point in the conversation, I do my best to engage the person in a way that builds the following dynamics, all of which are elements of a trusting connection:

Rapport. You may have heard this term used as an acronym: "Really all people prefer others reflecting them." Rapport develops when we show people that we understand them and their situation. I want the person in front of me to feel understood. I need them to hear me send the message, "I am going to listen well. I have no opinion or judgment about what has happened. I am not the cops, judge, jury, or your dad. I am actually on your side. I know this is a scary situation. I want to help you get to the real problem so you can be restored and strengthened as a result of this calamity."

Vulnerability. Trust can only be built through the exchange of truth. I need the person to be willing to step into the light and be seen. As I listen to them, I am going to see the truth—specifically, the truth of the internal problem that has led them to make this mess. I am going to ask them to show me parts of their heart that they might not know were there, to battle the fear and shame trying to keep them from showing me their true self. I'll see the truth before they do, so I need them the trust me to see it and do my best to lead them to the place where they can see it too. This will be scary, but when they see what I see, they will experience the power that comes from finally being able see the target, maybe for the first time in their life.

Responsibility. Trust is a choice that only a powerful person can make. I need the person to shift out of being an orphan and a powerless victim and grab hold of some newfound personal responsibility. At every point in this conversation, I am going to invite them to be powerful in trusting me, trusting God, trusting themselves, and trusting others.

Ultimately, I want to invite this person into a relational exchange that will function like a partnership. We will work together to find the problem that caused the mess and build an effective solution to it. When we emerge from this dark and scary place, we will have a new level of trust for each other. If we continue to walk together as the person executes the solution, we are likely to develop a deep connection, much like a doctor who walks through a pregnancy and delivery with a woman. It's impossible to experience a place of such vulnerability and trust together without forming a bond. Some of the people I know and love best are those I have walked with through cleaning up a mess. The good fruit of confrontation I have experienced in my life has not only removed my fear of stepping into a mess with someone—it has filled me with an enduring confidence and hope to see them radically transformed. I see it as an honor to serve them and get to know them intimately in the process.

Here's a basic checklist to review when approaching confrontation:

- What is my relationship with this person? What authority and trust do I have in their life? Do I need to borrow trust from someone to lower anxiety in this exchange?
- Am I prepared to go to this person in a spirit of gentleness—with no fear, anger, punishment, shame, or control?
- Is my goal in this exchange to show this person the Father by inviting them out of an orphan mentality and the punishment paradigm into their true identity as a son or daughter in the new covenant?
- Am I prepared to walk with this person through the repentance, reconciliation, and restoration process?

THE FIVE Es

In a confrontation, I use a basic roadmap for helping someone first discover the problem that caused their mess, and then build a plan for solving the problem and cleaning up the mess. I call it The Five Es:

1. EMPATHY: Lay the foundation for trust (rapport, vulnerability, responsibility)
2. EMPOWER: Introduce powerful questions to help the person take ownership of their mess and start searching for its root cause.
3. EXPLORE: Discover the root problem that led to the mess and who has been affected by it.
4. EDUCATE: Help the person build a plan for cleaning up their mess.
5. EXPECT: Create a target with goals and dates for when the mess will be cleaned up.

In order to reach each of these steps on the journey, these are the big questions I need them to answer:

1. EMPATHY: WHAT happened?
2. EMPOWER: WHAT is the problem and WHAT are you going to do about it?
3. EXPLORE: WHO is affected by this problem?
4. EDUCATE: WHAT are you willing to do to clean up this mess?
5. EXPECT: WHO will be helping you through this process and WHEN will I be convinced that this mess is cleaned up?

EMPATHY: WHAT HAPPENED?

My initial conversation with a person in a mess begins with me asking a question: "What happened?" Then I let the person spill all that they want to about the details of the incidents for which they were found out and brought to my office. Typically, I already know most of these details, but I want to listen to their version and discern as much as I can about how they're feeling and what they're thinking. As I listen, my first goal is to show empathy—to "feel with" them to demonstrate that I understand, I care, and I am here to partner with them, not oppose them.

One thing that usually becomes quickly obvious is that the person believes the reason they are there is to give a confession of their sins and be punished. Some people manifest this belief by displaying punishment-avoidance tactics—they clam up, become defensive, offer excuses, blame-shift, and even flat-out deny what they did. Others display compliance by offering a detailed confession of their sins, often punishing themselves in the process by declaring how bad and ashamed they are.

Unfortunately, many confrontations fail to lead people into repentance, reconciliation, and restoration because the person's expectation of punishment turns out to be realized. The first place this typically happens is when confession is mistaken for repentance. If we are satisfied when the person admits to the adultery, the porn addiction, the lying, or the backstabbing gossip, this is a clear sign that we are operating in the punishment paradigm. Remember, the punishment paradigm never requires repentance. It only requires a way to establish guilt, and that either comes through witness testimony or a confession. A confession authorizes us to punish and feel justified when we do. In a new covenant confrontation, however, a confession is only valuable in bringing the sin to the light so we can start looking for the problem.

One of the subtle ways people end up being punished in a confrontation is when the person confronting them starts telling them what they are or should be thinking and feeling, or how others are thinking and feeling. "Let me tell you what's going on. Let me tell you what you did. Let me tell you how destructive that was." It's like a parent scolding a child about their misdeeds. Genuine empathy involves identifying and validating what people are actually thinking and feeling. If we are afraid to validate someone's true feelings—because they are the offender and those feelings shouldn't matter, or because validating them is somehow approving of what they did—then we are going to operate with punishment instead of empathy.

Again, in order to approach someone in the "spirit of gentleness," we need to be spiritually and emotionally mature. This means we need to have spent time with the Father experiencing how He approaches us with empathy in our own sin: "For we do not have a high priest who is unable to empathize with our weaknesses, but we have one who has been tempted in every way, just as we are . . ." (Hebrews 4:15). He is not afraid of our mess. He is merciful and understanding. He knows exactly what we're going through. He is the safest place for us to confess what's happened. This is the truth we need to encounter for ourselves and show to others if we hope to win their trust and invite them to step into the light. If we can't offer this kind of empathy to someone, we need to go to the Father and learn from Him until we can.

Here are some common statements and questions I offer to show empathy:

- How are you feeling?
- This has got to be so scary.
- I can see that this hurts you so much.
- You've got to be feeling terrible about all this.
- Are you all right?
- Can I get you some water? Tissue?
- This has to be so hard to talk about.

Some obvious signs that my empathy is hitting the target is that I start being able to finish the person's sentences and they are nodding in agreement—we are understanding one another. I also see signs that their anxiety is dropping and they are feeling safer when they are able to look at me in the face, and their posture moves from closed to open.

EMPOWER: WHAT IS THE PROBLEM AND WHAT ARE YOU GOING TO DO ABOUT IT?

While the person is telling me what happened and I am empathizing with them in their situation, I am also asking myself, "What *really* happened?" I'm trying to get a 10,000-foot view of the situation and the person's behavior so I can see the patterns that point to the problem, because I don't yet know what the problem is.

I do know that the reason this person is in trouble—the adultery, drunk driving, lying, stealing, sexually acting out, etc.—is *not* the problem. These are the manifestations of the problem. I also know the reason the person hasn't truly repented is because they also do not know what the problem is. They may be sorry for their behavior—often they have done multiple rounds of getting caught, crying, confessing, apologizing, and managing to control it for a while before ending up right back in the same pig trough. With each failure, their hope for change has dwindled and the people in their lives have lost the ability to believe them. The problem is that they keep trying to repent for their behavior or its consequences. This is impossible. You can't repent of adultery, sex outside marriage, drunk driving, or pregnancy. You can feel terrible that you introduced these actions and consequences into your life and the lives of those around you, but you cannot make them go away.

The only way we can repent is to find and deal with the problem that led to the destructive behavior. Repentance is what leads to *conversion*:

> Repent therefore and be converted, that your sins may be blotted out, so that times of refreshing may come from the presence of the Lord . . . (Acts 3:19 NKJV)

Though we typically think of repentance and conversion as what we do when we give our lives to Jesus, they are ongoing practices in the Christian life. Repentance means to change your mind, and conversion is to change in form. This is what Paul describes in Romans 12:2: "Do not conform to the pattern of this world, but be transformed by the renewing of your mind." Or, as The Passion Translation puts it, "be inwardly transformed by the Holy Spirit through a total reformation of how you think." Repentance, not confession, is where the person breaks with the belief system, built on wounds and lies, that has led them to the affair, porn, lying, drunkenness, or gossip, and receives the truth that will set them free by forming a new mind and heart within them.

Now, I typically have a good hunch about what the problem might be, because the wounds and lies that produce bad beliefs and destructive behavior are very similar for all of us. At its foundation, all sin involves the same pattern. I know I am sitting in front of an orphan who has been trying to pursue their desires, meet their needs, or escape their fears in ways that violate God, themselves, and others. I know that shame, the fear of punishment, and the goal of self-preservation are driving their behavioral strategies. However, I am careful not to fall in the hole of jumping to conclusions (a lesson learned the hard way) about how and why that pattern is playing out in their lives. I also know the real challenge is going to be helping the person find and see the problem for themselves. This is why, even as I sit there stroking my beard and looking cool as a cucumber, I usually have a sense of inner desperation that is leading me to silently pray, "Jesus, help me. Help me. Help me. Oh God, I don't know what to do here. Help me see what's going on and find the problem. You said if anyone lacks wisdom he need only ask and You would give generously (James 1:5)." I press into the Holy Spirit by faith, trusting that He will enable me to listen to the person with prophetic wisdom and discernment and shine His light on the internal culture of their heart.

When the person concludes their initial "What happened" statement, I respond by asking, "So what is the problem?" This is where we really start to have an exchange back and forth, because finding the problem is where they most need my help. Some people will give an answer about behavior: "Well, the problem is that I cheated on my wife." Other people will admit, "I don't know what the problem is."

I start by asking more questions, such as:

- So why do you think you did that?
- What were you hoping to accomplish?
- What were you hoping to avoid?

- What are you so afraid of?
- What need were you trying to meet?
- Has this ever shown up before in your life?
- What did you do about it then?
- Did it work?
- If so, why is it back?
- Did you really find the problem the first time around?
- Do you know what the broken spot is?
- Do you know how other people experience you because of this broken place?

If their answer doesn't make sense or seems misleading, I will gently push back and ask them to try again. Commonly, this is where I begin to draw on my understanding of this person's DISC makeup, which allows me to see how this person interacts with their life and relationships. I will ask questions that get at their core needs, beliefs, motivations, and struggles. Eventually, as the pieces of information come together, I will start to suggest various interpretations to see if they land or not. "So, would you say this is why you did that? Is this what you were hoping would happen?" Sometimes I miss it and have to go back and pursue more information. Other times, I know I'm on track, but I need to rephrase it a few times before the person goes, "Yes, that sounds right." But eventually, if this part of the conversation is successful, we reach the point where I am able to hold up a picture of the problem that usually sounds something like this:

- "It sounds like you're afraid of being punished, humiliated, and disempowered. So your strategy for avoiding punishment is to never have any problems or need to ask anyone for help. You are living in hiding, even from yourself."

- "It sounds like you're afraid of being rejected for making a mistake or making someone unhappy. So your strategy is to avoid conflict and be perfect all the time."
- "It sounds like you're afraid of being destroyed and having everything taken from you. So you have made yourself king of your own castle, consolidated all the decision-making power, and surrounded yourself with people you can control and exploit."

If the person says, "No, that doesn't sound right," I'll rephrase it. Again, my goal is not to convince them of something before they see it for themselves. The money moment is when the light bulb goes on and the person goes, "You know what I'm doing? I'm living in hiding because I never want to let anyone see that I have problems. Because if they see me, I'll be punished, humiliated, and disempowered. That's why I've been so disconnected from my wife for so long and so out of touch with my own needs. That's why I got so desperate for connection that I betrayed my marriage."

Once the person sees the problem, it usually doesn't take them very long to see what I call the "broken spot"—the wounding experience, which they typically had in childhood, that introduced the lies on which their fear-driven, bad belief system was built. They start to connect the dots and understand that ever since that experience, they have been living out an orphan narrative that has shaped their behavior for a long time. Finding the broken spot is the most convincing evidence that you've correctly identified the problem—and points the way forward to the kind of repentance needed to solve the problem.

Finding the broken spot is also critical, because that's usually the point where the person gave their power away. They became a victim of their wound and the lies it taught them, and lost their sense of responsibility for their choices and the habits they were creating. The reason I call this the "Empower" step is that the person starts to unravel their victim mindset by becoming powerful in finding and owning their problem. When they start to answer my questions, I hear a lot of responses that sound like, "These things just happen to me. I don't understand. Women/men just keep hitting on me. I just went into this store and again I decided to steal something, and I got caught. It was just a beer. I think the cops are after me because my car is red—that's why they pulled me over." Each time I'll ask, "Okay, who decided that? Who made you do it? Who has the power to force you to do that? Who can control you?"

The message I'm sending in this exchange is, "You're a powerful person. You decide what you're going to do next. You look like you have some terrible habits, so it doesn't feel like you're deciding. You've been doing it so often, so regularly, that you have lost track of the fact that it's a decision you made. You've shortened the distance between cause and effect, and it feels like it's just happening. But you are choosing to get angry. You are choosing to use pot. You are choosing to search for pornography and masturbate. You are choosing to treat your spouse this way. The devil didn't make you do it. Neither did your parents, finances, race, gender, class, or any other person or circumstance. You're the one making these choices. The moment you recognize that is the moment you recognize that you are capable of choosing something different."

When we reach the point in the conversation where I hear the person essentially admit, "This is the problem, and I'm the one who put me in this mess," then I ask the next empowering question: "So what are you going to do?"

Often, they don't know what to do, so once again, I am there to help them search for the choice they want to make. I like to offer a few options and narrow it down. A couple options will be about what *not* to do: "Well, you could just keep doing what you've been doing and get sneakier about it. How would that work out for you?" The strong options will be things like seeking professional help from a counselor or psychologist, joining a twelve-step recovery group, or accessing certain books or other resources. The important thing is that they all involve a way for the person to receive healing for the broken spot, repent for the lies they've been believing, start to build a belief system based on the truth and begin to practice a new way and culture of being and behaving.

EXPLORE: WHO IS AFFECTED BY THIS PROBLEM?

Through the Empower stage, the person has taken their first steps out of the punishment paradigm. I do my best to show them the Father's heart—confronting shame with the message that they are a powerful and loved son or daughter, confronting the fear of punishment with gentleness, and confronting self-preservation with the invitation to choose connection. Once I see that the person is starting to make this journey by becoming powerful in finding their problem, I turn their attention to the mess—the wake of devastation they have caused to their connections with God, themselves, and others through their destructive behavior. This is the step where we really start to go after shifting out of the goal of self-preservation into pursuing the goal of connection.

I start by asking, "Who has been affected by this problem in your life?" I often use the "bucket of paint" analogy—"Imagine that you've dropped a bucket of paint and it has splashed on the people around you. Who has paint on them?"

One by one, the person will start to name those who have been most affected, usually starting with their most intimate relationships—God, their spouse, their family, their best friends. When they start to move further out in their circles of intimacy, I often will make suggestions and remind them of people who most likely have been affected. Typically, there are people at work, at church, in the community, or other places where they have influence who have paint on them and need to be acknowledged.

With each of these people and groups, I invite the person to think specifically about how the mess has affected them or will affect them once they find out about it. It's at this point, when face after face begins to flash before the person's eyes and they finally allow themselves to see and feel the damage they've caused, that godly sorrow kicks in. Tears start to flow as they realize, "Oh my gosh. What have I done? How did I let this happen? I have hurt all these people."

I camp here for as long as I can, because godly sorrow is so critical to repentance: "For godly sorrow produces repentance leading to salvation, not to be regretted; but the sorrow of the world produces death" (2 Corinthians 7:10 NKJV). Most of these people have experienced plenty of worldly sorrow, which is part of the punishment paradigm. It's the painful shame of being caught. It's the "woe is me" whining of the victim. It's the tearful apologies and begging for people to let you off without cleaning up your mess. Worldly sorrow leads to death because it's ultimately self-focused and only leads you further down the orphan path. It's just more fruit of the broken spot and its lies. But godly sorrow is the fruit of finally seeing the truth of who God is, who you are, and how you have devalued and damaged the most valuable things in your life—your relational connections. It's grief that you have not loved God and others as they deserve. And it's this grief that finally breaks your heart in a way that leads you to say, "These people need more than an apology from me. They need a new me. I never want to cause this kind of pain to us again. What do I need to do to clean up the mess and change so that I never make this kind of mess again?"

EDUCATE: WHAT ARE YOU WILLING TO DO TO CLEAN UP THIS MESS?

Once I see that the person has really understood the extent of the mess they've made, I will ask, "So what do you want to do to clean up this mess?" When I hear them say, "I will do whatever it takes. I'm willing to do whatever I have to do to ensure that this never happens again," then I know we are ready to move forward with the next step of the process, which is building a plan to clean up the mess.

I like to build this plan around the list of people, organized in concentric circles or levels of intimacy, that we compiled during the Explore step.

Again, I start by asking them questions. "What do you want to do to clean up your mess with God? With yourself? With your spouse? With your children? With the leaders in your life?" I know that they are going to need to have a conversation, either in person or in writing, with each of these people, and I invite them to consider the specific damage they've caused to that relationship and what they need to apologize and ask forgiveness for.

Often, I will coach the person on how to prepare for those conversations. I'll ask, "What are you going to tell them that is different so that they believe that this will never happen to anyone else in your future? Do you think they will believe you?" My goal is that through this discussion, the person will get the clarity and courage they need to step into the conversation ready to say three things:

1. This is what I did. I have betrayed and damaged our connection. I'm deeply grieved that I have done this and I want to do anything I can to clean up my mess with you. Please forgive me.
2. What do you need from me to clean up this mess?

3. This is my plan for fixing my problem so that I don't make this mess again. I invite your feedback as I walk out this plan so I can know how you're experiencing me and if I'm changing like I want to.

I also encourage the person to be an assertive communicator. "You're going to be talking to some hurting people," I tell them, "and they're probably going to say some stuff that's going to rock your world. Accept responsibility for your part. Don't accept responsibility for what they decide to do. If they become bitter, judgmental, and punishing, do not take responsibility for that. You are not a prisoner in front of a firing squad. You are two powerful people working through a very painful situation. You didn't come there so they could hurt you back—you came to clean up the mess."

Here are my basic guidelines for cleaning up a mess:

1. You'd better know the problem that you are fixing.
2. You need to know how to fix it or have a convincing clue.
3. Have a plan that includes several other people, credible people.
4. Understand how others have experienced you in your problem.
5. Listen to them, allow them to show you their pain.
6. Own the pain you've caused.
7. Convince the people you've hurt that this problem is solved and won't be coming around again.
8. Ask for forgiveness.
9. Keep your love on throughout this process.
10. Be patient.

EXPECT: WHO WILL BE HELPING YOU THROUGH THIS PROCESS? WHEN WILL I BE CONVINCED THAT THIS MESS IS CLEANED UP?

The Educate step is complete when the person has both parts of their plan intact and knows what they are going to do. Part 1 is what they will do to work on themselves to fix the problem, and Part 2 is what they will do to clean up the mess with the people in their lives. The final step in the confrontation process is to establish accountability, determine the timeline, and define success as they carry out their plan. Here are some questions I typically ask during the Expect stage:

- Do you need anything from me?
- Do you want me to be part of this process?
- Who will you get help from besides me?
- Who will you be accountable to besides me?
- How will I know how you are doing in your work with that person?
- At what point do I find out how you're doing? Date?
- When does this mess get cleaned up?

I never require the person to make me their primary coach, guide, or accountability in this process. If I have been successful in building trust with the person through this conversation, I know I will likely be on the list of people they want help from. But they may have a counselor, therapist, pastor, friend, or other helper they trust and want to work with. If this is the case, I just need them to convince me that the person will actually help and empower them to walk out the process and plan we've made together. I want to hear that this person will expect them to be powerful and responsible, help them see the choices they're making, and help them see what they can change and what's not their responsibility to change. I don't want them to pick someone who will fall into the classic boss-employee, pastor-parishioner, leader-follower, or parent-child dynamic of, "This person is in trouble and deserves to be controlled for a while."

The classic problem with "accountability groups" is that they either become too controlling or too lax because they don't require people to stop being victims and become powerful. They don't help people find their problems and broken spots so they can repent and change. They are either places where people say, "Please stop me from pooping my pants," or "We just commiserate about how we can't stop pooping our pants." Healthy accountability is where we go, "I am going to stop pooping my pants and I would appreciate your support in helping me make that choice."

The timeline will usually involve stages and need a level of flexibility to accommodate people's schedules and the different paces at which people clean up the mess. In Ben Armstrong's case, he was having conversations with people for up to two years after his affair became public because his confession was shared globally, and he made an open invitation for anyone who needed to talk to him to approach him. Talk about courage and commitment to cleaning up his mess! Often, decisions will need to be part of the plan, such as whether this person keeps their job, or whether the spouse files for divorce. However, it's important that the plans have dates to keep them moving forward.

In the next three chapters, we will look in more detail at what a successful journey of repentance, reconciliation, and restoration looks like. But at this point in the journey, the person should have enough information to start envisioning the fruit of genuine repentance and conversion in their lives. The fruit of repentance is always radical transformation. You think differently. You speak differently. You live differently. You choose differently. You're a brand-new person. As a result, "times of refreshing" come from the Lord to you and everything in your life—your meditations, beliefs, character, words, choices, habits, relationships, marriage, and work. That's what a cleaned-up mess looks like, and that's what both the person and those around them should expect to see. We should hear reports that the old patterns of behavior are giving way to new behaviors of trust, peace, and connection. If the person starts reverting to their old behavior, then we need to go see where deeper repentance is needed.

When the person leaves my office, the last thing they hear from me is that I believe in them. I believe they have a plan that is going to work, and I am cheering them on as they execute it. I believe they are repenting, and that their repentance will be completed. I believe they are walking out of my office in the power of the Holy Spirit, who is partnering with them to build a brand-new life. And I believe one day soon we will all be rejoicing at the incredible fruit of a life transformed by repentance, reconciliation, and restoration.

CHAPTER 8

REPENTANCE

During a recent ministry trip to the UK, Sheri and I saw the Broadway musical *The Lion King* in London. The production was simply spectacular. The costumes were wonderfully creative, and the performers were out-of-this-world talented. But the most powerful thing of all was the story. It's a story of repentance, reconciliation, and restoration—in fact, it's the prodigal son story.

Simba, son and heir of Mufasa, king of the Pride Lands, is derailed from his destiny when his uncle Scar (his name is a perfect metaphor for the wounds that introduce the "broken spot" into our lives) blames him for his father's death and sends him into exile. Running from his shame, he lives a life of *hakuna matata* ("no worries"—no responsibility) as an orphan in the jungle with his friends.

Then one day, his old friend Nala shows up, reminds him of his true identity and responsibility to be king, and describes the devastation that has occurred to his kingdom in his absence (a great picture of the collateral damage we cause when we live in sin as a victim of our wounds). Simba doesn't respond well to Nala's confrontation, and after she leaves, he keeps trying to spin in denial to ward off the uncomfortable truths she's raised. "She's wrong. I can't go back. What would it prove anyway? It won't change anything. You can't change the past."

This internal conversation is interrupted by the Rafiki (a type of the Holy Spirit), who leads Simba into another confrontation. Instead of trying to convince Simba to agree with him, however, Rafiki talks to him in riddles and questions. When Simba asks, "Who are you?" Rafiki responds, "The question is, who are you?"

"Oh, I suppose you know," says Simba.

"Sure do. You're Mufasa's boy. Bye!"

Rafiki takes off, requiring Simba to chase his answer. When Simba catches up and asks, "You knew my father?" Rafiki replies, "Correction. I know your father." Simba tries to explain that his father is dead, but Rafiki insists, "He's alive! I'll show him to you." He then leads Simba on another chase through a tangled root system of trees and soggy marshland to a reflection pool (an apt image for a self-discovery process). When Simba says, "All I see is my reflection," Rafiki presses, "Look harder. He lives . . . in you."

Suddenly, Simba begins to have a vision of his father. The sky opens and Mufasa appears in the clouds telling him, "Simba, you have forgotten me . . . You have forgotten who you are, and so have forgotten me. Look inside yourself, Simba. You are more than what you have become . . . You are my son, and the one true king. Remember who you are."

After the vision fades, Rafiki comes to him asking more questions. "What was that?"

Simba starts to process what it will mean to walk out his repentance. "I know what I have to do. But going back means I'll have to face my past. I've been running from it for so long."

"The way I see it, you can either run from it or learn from it," Rafiki offers. Then he asks the powerful question: *"So, what are you going to do?"*

"I'm going back," Simba decides, and takes off.

"Good! Go on!" Rafiki calls after him, howling with laughter. "Get out of here!"

The rest of the story shows that Simba's repentance was genuine. He returns to his land, defeats Scar, and takes his rightful place as king. As a result, his subjects, his kingdom, and his legacy are all restored.[13]

RELATIONAL IDENTITY

This story captures the nature of genuine repentance so beautifully. We see Simba's mindset shifting out of the punishment paradigm and into a new covenant paradigm. His shame gives way to worthiness, his fear of punishment to love and courage, and his self-preservation to connection, all of which produce a radical shift in behavior from irresponsibility and isolation to running toward his relational responsibilities. But what *The Lion King* especially gets right is that at the heart of every repentance journey, the pivotal experience we must have is to remember the Father and remember who we really are. We see this in the parable of the prodigal son:

> But when he came to himself, he said, "How many of my father's hired servants have bread enough and to spare, and I perish with hunger! I will arise and go to my father, and will say to him, 'Father, I have sinned against heaven and before you, and I am no longer worthy to be called your son. Make me like one of your hired servants.'" (Luke 15:17-19 NKJV)

The prodigal son "came to himself"—that is, remembered who he was—as he remembered his father. It was this act of remembering his

[13] *The Lion King*, directed by Roger Allers and Rob Minkoff, (Walt Disney Pictures, 1994).

relational identity that freed him from his prison of shame and set him on the path home.

At the center of every "broken spot" in our lives is a false narrative about the world and our place in it that leads us to take on a false, shame-based identity. Some of us, like Simba, heard a message that we were to blame for something bad happening, and so we couldn't be trusted with power. Others of us heard the message that we couldn't trust that our needs would be met by others and had to take care of ourselves. A great number of us heard the message that our value lay in our talent, intelligence, good looks, possessions, prestige, accomplishments, or some other characteristic, and so our only hope of security and worth lay in developing and preserving these things. Every one of these shame-based identity narratives leads us to operate within the punishment paradigm. The only way out of the punishment paradigm is to replace those narratives with the truth. The real shift we make in repentance is not merely changing our core beliefs, goals, and behavioral strategies, but our fundamental identity.

There is only one place that effectively contradicts the lie of shame that our flaws make us unworthy of connection, one source of true, eternal value and worth that cannot be stolen or lost through any circumstance or choice, and that is our relationship with the Father. Making our home in His love and living in our relational identity as His sons and daughters is what delivers us from the punishment paradigm. This is why the "joy set before" Jesus was not merely taking our punishment or forgiving our sin but reconciling us to the Father—that was the reason He "endured the cross" (Hebrews 12:2). This is why the genuine fruit of the gospel in our lives is not that we go to church or read our Bibles or pray—it is that we learn to think, act, and live in absolutely every way like a true son or daughter of the Father.

One thing *The Lion King* and other fictional stories leave out, however—even Jesus' parable—is that the timeline for confronting someone and helping lead them to repentance, or for them to experience their own divine confrontation and turnaround, is rarely the work of a moment, a day, or a week. Even the Five Es model I introduced in Chapter 7 is not one I always get to execute in its entirety in one conversation in my office. Sometimes it needs to happen in a series of conversations over a period of time. Sometimes confronting someone in a mess, offering them a place to repent, and watching to see what they're going to do is a process that unfolds over weeks and months.

The challenge for those of us who are inviting people into this journey is that we must be consistent in offering them a place to repent while being prepared to introduce appropriate boundaries and consequences if they don't. As I said in Chapter 2, the problem in punishment-based environments is that we simply don't give people a place to repent, or if they do repent, we insist that they still be punished. In the new covenant, we must create a place for repentance while also communicating clearly the consequences of not repenting. One of the things that makes this difficult is that repentance is not some formula we can walk people through—it's a gift they receive from the Father. All we can do is invite and urge them to pursue this gift, with confidence that if they seek it, the Father will be faithful to give it.

THE HOT MESS OF JONATHAN WELTON

Several years ago, I had the opportunity to meet and get to know a young, gifted Bible teacher and theologian, Jonathan Welton, and his wife, Karen. Sheri and I immediately hit it off with them, and it wasn't long before we were taking steps to share our resources and partner in ministry in a variety of ways. He had read my books and was eager to have me bringing the message of healthy, honoring relationships and culture to the students of his online Bible school, Welton Academy. I appreciated his teaching on covenant theology, which contained many fresh insights that informed my own understanding. In particular, his teaching on the five covenants of the Bible, and his theology of the new covenant—he calls it Better Covenant theology—informed much of my thinking and approach in Chapters 4 and 5 of this book. Little did I know that our friendship and partnership was positioning me to walk with the Weltons through one of the greatest challenges of their lives.

In August of 2018, a couple of ministry leader friends reached out to say that they had been involved in a series of unsuccessful confrontations with Jonathan over some reports of inappropriate and immoral behavior, and asked me to get involved. As the confrontation process unfolded, we experienced many of the classic ups, downs, roadblocks, and breakthroughs that I have commonly seen in people's repentance journeys, so I asked Jonathan and Karen if they would be willing to let me present the story as a case study in this book. They agreed.

My ministry friends informed me that in late 2017, several women on staff at Welton Academy had come forward with complaints that he was behaving inappropriately towards some of the female staff members at the school. A member of Jonathan's advisory leadership team called a meeting with Jonathan and the staff members to address these concerns, during which he apologized. Subsequently, he had met with three of the staff members and again confessed that their concerns were valid and apologized. Six months later, however, his office manager reported to another member of the advisory leadership that Jonathan's behavior had not changed, and had even escalated to the point where, among the staff, dealing with it was becoming "cultural."

When I reached out to Jonathan to ask if what my friends were telling me was true, he told me that he had been having misunderstandings with his staff, but that they were manageable and not as serious as what these leaders were making them out to be. However, when I checked his story with a pastor couple closely connected with Jonathan's ministry, they told me that the reports they were hearing were much more serious and alarming than he had made out and asked for my help and input on how to deal with the situation. I then had a follow-up call with one of the leaders who had originally contacted me. He shared more details of the reports he had confirmed, which immediately revealed that there could be grounds for at least five women to file sexual harassment charges against Jonathan if they chose. This leader explained that he had tried to confront Jonathan and it had not gone well, which had prompted him to resign from Jonathan's advisory team and write a letter to some of the Welton Academy students he had been mentoring explaining why he would no longer be involved in the school. I then called another member of Jonathan's advisory team, who told me that the reports he had been hearing matched those of the newly resigned leader.

I should mention that early in my relationship with Jonathan, he shared some of his background with me. Nearly a decade earlier, when he and Karen were newly married, he had had a brief affair. At the time, he was traveling and ministering publicly through an apostolic network where he had previously interned. When he confessed the infidelity, the leaders of the network explained that he would need to go through a "restoration" process to maintain his credentialing with them. This process included limited accountability and oversight with one of the leaders who checked in with him periodically as he and Karen scrambled to pick up the pieces of their marriage. They read some of my books and did their best to put them to work in rebuilding vulnerability and trust. Eventually, the leaders gave him a "yellow light" to return to ministry.

With all this evidence on the table, I knew we had a serious situation on our hands. It was clear to me that Jonathan had not successfully repented and healed the broken spot behind his immoral behavior after the first affair. Instead, a stronghold of self-deception had grown inside him to match the ministry kingdom he had built outside him—a kingdom where he had all the power and could not be confronted, and therefore where he was capable of inflicting much greater damage. I knew it was time for him to be presented with consequences if he refused to recognize the size and impact of the mess he had been creating. In my mind, an unrepentant Jonathan could mean leaving hundreds of walking wounded in his wake for years to come. At the same time, I also carried hope that he could join the ranks of those leaders I had seen do a great job of repenting, cleaning up their mess, and restoring their relationships.

CONFRONTATION AND CONSEQUENCES

As it happened, the timing of this confrontation coincided with a personal illness. A major flare-up of gout in both my feet and left knee, along with a case of bronchitis, put me on the couch for two weeks with nothing else to do than address Jonathan's situation. In that time, I ended up spending close to thirty-five hours on the phone, Skype, and email moving the confrontation and discipline process forward.

First, I called Jonathan and Karen, presented them with the reports I had heard from his pastors and advisory leaders, and asked, "So what happened?" Jonathan denied everything that didn't have incontrovertible evidence in an email or text thread, and tried to minimize what he couldn't deny into something harmless. This led us into a truth-finding process that involved at least fifteen hours of calls between Jonathan, me, his pastors, advisory team, and staff. Through this investigation, the evidence against him became more shatterproof, and his pattern of lying and denial became visible to everyone except him. He also displayed a willingness to discredit and dishonor everyone confronting him . . . except me. With me he remained accessible, engaged, and cooperative—to the point where he agreed to my request that he allow a Christian psychiatrist to perform a psychological evaluation on him.

After Jonathan received the results of his evaluation and learned that he fit the profile for clinical covert narcissism, he wrote a letter to his advisory leaders in which he apologized for his behavior and announced that he was stepping down from his position as president of the Academy. When I read this letter, I noticed that it was full of shame and self-punishment, but wanted to believe that much of his remorse was sincere:

> I am absolutely ashamed of my behavior and the hurt that I have caused. I have abused the trust of any person around me that would consider themselves friends. I abused spiritual language for my own benefit and preyed upon those that believed me to be a safe leader for them. But I am not safe and I have created something that has caused massive pain to the people that have loved me the most. I have selfishly built a system, which allowed me to exist this way without question . . . I was so manipulative of others that I even deceived myself and found ways to justify to myself the violation of my friendships . . .
>
> I am choosing to submit to correction in my life. Effective immediately, I resign from being the President of Welton Academy, and hand the reins to my advisor board. The best thing for those that have believed in me and cheered me on is for me to step aside from the public eye and seek professional counseling and begin to clean up my mess.

However, less than a week after Jonathan sent out this letter, it came to light that he had involved one of his staff members in an elaborate plan to cover up indiscretions he'd committed with her. This exposure made it clear to me that his letter had nothing to do with genuine repentance. It was a crafted apology that imitated conviction and empathy for his victims, using the language of people who had confronted him, with the goal of convincing them that he had punished himself and did not need to be punished by them. It was now abundantly clear to me that it was time to set a limit with a man who was not going to or was unable to repent.

With Jonathan's approval, I reached out to the leaders who had been involved in the process so far and asked if they would be willing to join me in forming an advisory board to determine, communicate, and enforce appropriate consequences for Jonathan's behavior. I then drafted and sent out a letter with the board's approval to the Welton Academy students, the school's credentialing organization, and a group of selected leaders. In it I laid out the list of consequences we were recommending, which included accepting Jonathan's resignation and requiring him to seek psychiatric help, establishing a no-contact policy between him and his staff, closing the school and refunding every student's tuition, and compensating every staff member with up to six months of income and counseling services. I explained that the board had spiritual authority only, not legal authority, and as sole proprietor of the school, Jonathan was still free to act as he chose. I was also clear that while these consequences were necessary given Jonathan's lack of repentance, we were still praying and working to invite him into a place to repent:

> It grieves me to write this letter knowing the ramifications. This entire advisory board is friends with Jonathan and Karen. The staff at the Welton Academy, even those chased away, are rooting for his successful turnaround. As of the writing of this letter, Jon is making slow if any progress. Repentance is not clear and thus the warning you hear in this letter. No repentance, no change. That reality creates an ongoing expectation of more of the same. Jon is not fit to be a leader, nor is he safe to have access to other people's vulnerability . . . He is not yet able to convince anyone around him that he's broken over

> what he's done to so many and has absolutely no credibility when he speaks.
>
> There are numerous people victimized in this situation, none of them are named Jonathan. Up to now, he has spun all of his responsibility outward. Will we see Jon own this enormous mess, change into a new man and reconcile with the many people who love and believe in him? Time will tell. I pray that God has mercy and grants repentance to my good friend, Jonathan Welton.

I spoke to Jonathan on the phone on the day this letter went out. He told me he thought the letter was fair and thanked me for it. When I spoke to Karen later, however, I found her quite agitated and on the verge of panic, which was quite understandable. Until I had stepped in to help bring the facts to light, she'd been trusting Jonathan's false stories about what he had been doing and what all these confrontations were really about. She was still reeling from the revelation that she'd once again been the victim of her husband's betrayal and deceit, but this time they had so much more to lose. Shutting down the school and making payouts to the students and staff had the potential to financially ruin their family. She was eight months pregnant with their third child, and they had just bought a new home. She was desperate for hope and wisdom for how she needed to proceed in the situation.

I emphasized to Karen that Jonathan did not yet know he had a problem, much less what it was. I was convinced that he was not going to wake up to reality until, as I put it, his "misery becomes greater than his fear." Until he found repentance, everyone around him needed to adjust their relationship with him—starting with her. At this point, she had already kicked him and all his things out of the house to send the message that he had a serious problem that he needed to work on. A few weeks later, the psychiatrist who had evaluated Jonathan recommended that they establish a ninety-day therapeutic separation agreement with the mutual goal of reconciliation, in order to reduce the anxiety in the relationship and establish healthy boundaries. I voiced my support for this plan and did my best to encourage Karen that God would take care of her family and suggest ways for her to set healthy boundaries and focus on her own healing during this season.

FINDING THE PROBLEM

As I'd hoped, being kicked out of his house and facing the prospect of losing his family on top of his ministry seemed to spur Jonathan to action like nothing else. Learning that he had covert narcissistic tendencies, which meant he had a fragile/terrified inner self and was creating a false self as a protection mechanism for the outer world to see, had done a lot to break through his denial, but these realities did a lot to shatter his illusion that he still had control and could somehow maneuver through these consequences and come out intact. He moved in with his parents, took jobs as a handyman, and began to pursue several resources to get help. He had daily sessions with an inner healing counselor, received a few days of intensive counseling at a center in Seattle that dealt specifically with narcissism, and began attending a twelve-step recovery group for sex addiction to be around men who knew how to be vulnerable and honest about their mistakes.

About six weeks after sending out the disciplinary letter, I was able to meet with Jonathan and Karen in person for about three hours. I asked him to fill me in on the steps he'd been taking to find and work on his problem and what progress he had made. He did his best to show me that he was doing everything he could to find the problem and repent. However, as I began to ask questions and give feedback, I saw that he still could not resist the habit of trying to minimize, avoid, or deny the picture of his problem I was trying to show him. And I knew that the only reason he would still be doing this, and the only reason for the intensity of the addictive cycles he had constantly pounding through his heart, mind, and soul, were because he was still in the grip of some deep terror at his core. He still hadn't found his real problem or repented for it.

So, I began to press him. "What are you so afraid of, Jon? You're a man who has built a castle, surrounded it with a moat, and only allowed people in you think you can control, or who will leave. When people try to confront you, you lie and deny your face off. Here's what I think. I think you are terrified of being destroyed, disempowered, and stripped of your role as a credible teacher and influencer."

Jon's immediate response was, "I don't think that feels true to me." But in the weeks that followed, he began to ponder my words. When I talked with him later, he explained that after our conversation he began to ask himself, "What am I repenting for? Am I repenting of narcissism? Sex addiction? Deception and lying? And I began to see that all of these were rooted in the fear of being destroyed. That fear was wired to everything I did—all my thinking, all my actions. That was why my love sucked. That was why I wasn't being open, honest, vulnerable, accountable, or trusting anybody. I had just been trying to cut the fruit off that tree my whole life. Now I knew I needed to go after that root."

Jon had finally found his problem. However, he still wasn't clear about what that meant or what needed to happen next. At some point in mid-November, he asked me if I thought he had repented.

"I think you're repenting," I answered.

"What does that mean?" he asked.

"You're showing signs that you know what it means to repent and even that you know what the problem is. But you still need to find and heal the broken spot. And you're just starting to figure out what it will mean to put a plan together that will convince anyone that you're actually going to change."

Jon took this information back to his counselor and they began to go after the broken spot that had introduced the root of fear in his life. Through this process, they discovered that from very early in his childhood, he had determined that being emotionally vulnerable meant extreme danger, and that the only way to feel safe was to be the smartest person in the room. This caused him to bury and protect his heart and project a false self into the world, which had only produced false relational connections and emotional starvation. He finally began to recognize how completely disconnected from God and his own heart he had lived his entire life due to this fear. He'd never been able to connect to his feelings or express his needs. He'd never been able to form deep bonds of trust with other people in which he felt safe to practice vulnerability. He saw more clearly than ever that the relational culture he had built with God, with himself, and with every person in his life was defined by the goal of self-preservation. His entire life, he had been running from the truth and maneuvering to get his needs met and stay in control.

There was a deep and tragic irony in these discoveries, because Jonathan had built his entire ministry on teaching and preaching the "better covenant" theology that through Christ, we have been brought into a covenant of forgiveness and reconciled to the Father as beloved sons and daughters. Significantly, the leader who had disciplined him after his first affair had urged him that the key to his repentance and restoration was to become a son—and he was right. But instead of actually becoming a son through the radical inner work of healing, repentance, and renewing his mind, Jonathan had dedicated his life to studying and proclaiming the message of sonship. He was like a child who endlessly dreamed of visiting Disneyland, studied everything there is to know about Disneyland, and talked every day to his friends about how awesome Disneyland is, without ever going to Disneyland. He longed for nothing more than to live in the reality of the Father's love and experience the beauty of new covenant relationships, yet he couldn't see that the fruit of his life revealed that he was still an orphan at heart. In many ways, he was like the apostle Paul, full of zeal for the covenant of God, yet completely unaware that he is a self-righteous, murderer who is directly attacking the God and people he proclaims to love. Paul needed a radical confrontation with Jesus, a few days of blindness, and the help of a brave friend before the scales fell from his eyes. Jonathan's blindness seemed to last for months, but eventually, his sight began to clear as Jesus shone the light of truth on his heart.

Jonathan's counselor provided a description of his inner healing journey that Jon graciously shared with me. It beautifully describes some of the steps of inner healing, renewing of the mind, and spiritual deliverance people classically take on their journey of repentance. The counselor describes four significant stages of Jonathan's healing—childhood trauma, torment, self-acceptance, and a broken heart:

> Childhood trauma.
> As Jonathan and I walked through his childhood, I had the privilege of facilitating Jesus into place after place in his mind. Memory after memory. I watched Jesus not only heal Jonathan's heart through the mind renewal process I do, but also re-parent Jonathan's heart to feel what it never got to feel in secure protected love. To make heart connections with the Father that left Jonathan feeling loved, safe, protected and cared for. These moments of healing and mind renewal began to give Jonathan an ability to see relationships from a position of vulnerability rather than defensive protection. A place of safety and security rather than fear and hiding. He began to open and come alive as Jesus was making his heart alive. He began to understand that vulnerability was a strength to be pursued rather than a

weakness to be shunned. I began to see him start to see things from others' perspectives and began to feel empathy for others and what they were going through because of his actions and decisions based on his brokenness.

Torment.

Another significant turn came as a genuine deliverance came to Jonathan. As we were praying in one of our sessions . . . Jonathan had a tangible inner and outer reaction to the prayer. Physically, he had a reaction (NOT to be confused with a manifestation) that released some things in his physical body. Internally, he had a bigger and more significant reaction. His mind was quiet, calm, and clear. He "had not ever known this kind of clarity of mind or peace" in his life. The results were amazing. He was and remains profoundly calm and peaceful. His mind still carries that clarity. He never realized that a large group of his thoughts and feelings were not his own, but this tormenting spirit leading him to believe it was always him. The peace and posture of ease were not only noticeable immediately to me but also others whom he engaged almost immediately after that session.

Self-acceptance.

After the "dust" cleared from the tormenting, the direction seemed to shift to a light on Jonathan's heart in the area of self-acceptance. Specifically, understanding what he had done to people and the effects his action and life had done in others' lives. I saw what I believe to be a godly sorrow start to emerge as he wondered in his realization why anyone would want to stay in his life with the way he had conducted himself. He also processed through the need to forgive himself for his own peace and be able to listen and show care for other's hearts needed to express themselves to him.

> I watched the Holy Spirit walk him through letting go of his own rejection of himself so that he can now accept the hurt and pain he caused in others as they express it to him.
>
> A broken heart.
> Our last major turn of the heart to this point came when Jesus opened up the deep wounds of Jonathan's first love relationship and rejections. Jonathan's heart had been hurt beyond natural repair. Jesus came into his pain and released him from it. Jesus spoke truth to his heart and brought his heart back online where Jonathan had pulled way back from any further intimacy and vulnerability by vaulting it down with three deep-seated vows that were holding him captive: "I will not be vulnerable, I will not trust, and I won't let anyone in this close again." I believe this healing may have the biggest implications positively to not only saving his marriage but causing it to thrive.[14]

Uprooting shame and fear in Jonathan's heart didn't happen in a moment. He spent several more months of counseling and inner healing allowing the Holy Spirit to expose the lies he had believed for so long and speak truth to his heart. It was in these months that he finally remembered himself and remembered the Father, began to come home to his true identity, and finally began to shift inside from punishment to the new covenant paradigm. And it soon became evident to me, Karen, and others, that Jon was finally making progress in his repentance journey. We were seeing signs of a new Jonathan, one who was starting to connect to the thoughts, feelings, and needs in his heart, act vulnerable, and build a solid plan for cleaning up his mess.

---

[14] Board update letter on behalf of Jonathan Welton, written by Nathan Blouse, Therapist with The Safe Place Ministries.

THE QUESTION

In the next chapter, I'll continue Jonathan and Karen's story and describe how Jonathan began the process of reconciliation with God, himself, and others. But here I want to re-emphasize two critical points about the journey of repentance.

First, we must resist the temptation to be satisfied with confession and apologies. Telling all the gory details of what you did is not repentance—it's just a way for other people to feel better about punishing you. "Sorry" is not repentance—it's just a request to do it again. Neither confession nor apologies lead to change, because they never get to the problem.

Second, if we want to make a place for people to repent and know with certainty when they have repented, then we must ensure that we help them find the problem and fix the broken spot. As we see in Jonathan's case, this often requires repeated confrontation. Jon himself admitted, "Confrontation that requires repentance is so important because of the self-deceiving nature of sin. I was confronted over and over, but because my heart was caged within me and had become hard, I couldn't see or feel what I was doing wrong. I could only mentally comprehend and confess to the things pointed out to me. But when those confronting me weren't satisfied, it set me on the path to discover that I couldn't repent without having an engaged heart. That was when the deception finally started to break."

Repentance is the choice we need to see people make, and it will be clear when they do, because they will change. They will bear fruit of repentance, which means they will move from an orphan to a son or daughter, from shame to worthiness, from fear to love, from self-preservation to connection. They don't just stop the bad behavior—they start to build a new life of healthy, loving, safe, truth-filled connection with God, themselves, and others.

When people ask me, "How do you know if someone has repented?" I ask them, "How do you know if someone is saved?" When someone is born again, no one around them asks, "I wonder if they were born again." If you have a genuine repentance and conversion, then the angels are rejoicing, and so are those closest to you!

Once we learn to invite and expect genuine repentance, it becomes pretty straightforward to see when someone is choosing not to repent. And the person who doesn't repent when confronted is really the easiest person to deal with. I like to ask, "How many pet rattlesnakes do you have?" The answer: none. "So how many intimate relationships do you have with scary people in them?" None. "How many scary people do you have on your leadership team?" None. The unrepentant person is unsafe and needs boundaries. Boundaries are different than walls. Walls communicate fear and rejection—they are a form of punishment. Boundaries are a limit set to protect the value of something. When someone starts to devalue their relationship through irresponsibility and disrespect, a boundary says, "I require high levels of respect and responsibility in my relational connections. I need you to adjust and clean up your mess so we can restore connection. If you refuse to do that, you are demonstrating that you can no longer be trusted with the place of access and intimacy I've given you." Boundaries communicate the hope of reconciliation.

Setting boundaries with an unrepentant person is something we must do in the spirit of gentleness, just as we confront. If we are filled with fear or anger, we will either back down from setting healthy limits or turn them into tools of punishment. To set boundaries well, we need to be like Nala or Rafiki—able to see and remind someone who's acting like an absolute orphan that even though they are blind with self-deception and fear, the truth of who they are remains. They are a loved son or daughter of the Father. Even if they choose to run from Him, from themselves, and from we who love them, we will all be holding on to the truth and waiting and watching for their return.

CHAPTER 9

RECONCILIATION

Have you ever witnessed a miracle? I have friends and colleagues who have seen countless tumors disappear, deaf ears open, and blind eyes receive sight before their eyes. In my life, however, one of the most dramatic miracles I've ever watched unfold was a reconciliation that took place in my office over a decade ago.

A couple was on the brink of divorce because the husband had ended up in bed with the wife's best friend.[15] It was the second time he had committed adultery in their marriage. Sheri and I sat across from them with utter certainty that only divine intervention could save this devastated relationship. And then it happened. In a moment, God revealed to this man the broken spot in his life, a wound from childhood caused by his father. The man forgave his father and broke his agreement with the lie that had brought so much destruction to his heart and connections. The next moment, he was healed and changed. He began looking around the room like a blind man who had just received sight, and the first person he saw was his wife.

He looked into her eyes and said fervently, "I love you so much!" This was the first sign of his transformation—in eighteen years of mar-

---

[15] I tell this story in more detail in my book *Culture of Honor*.

riage, he had hardly ever told his wife he loved her. "I cannot believe you are still here after what I have put you through," he continued. "I am so sorry. Will you forgive me?"

"Yes," his wife nodded, weeping. "I have prayed for this day to come. I forgive you."

There wasn't a dry eye in the room. We could hardly believe it. It's the only time I've seen it happen like that in all my years working with people. But it was absolutely real. That couple has been living in a restored relationship full of love and connection ever since that day. Their testimony constantly reminds me of what the new covenant makes possible for those of us who believe.

Now, most of the time watching people repent, clean up their mess, forgive, and reconcile their relationships is like watching a flower bloom. We are still seeing God's gifts of repentance and forgiveness at work in people's lives—it just takes time, patience, faith, and hope. If you happen to be one of the people with "paint" on them from somebody's mess, these qualities can be challenging to come by. One of the reasons we so often end up reacting to people's sin with punishment is that we feel a righteous urgency for them to clean up their mess with the people they've hurt, without understanding what that requires. Instead of making room for genuine repentance and transformation, we rush into making them do something to pay for their crime and balance the scales of justice.

What we need to understand is that genuine repentance and reconciliation honor God's design for the priority of relationships in our lives. As we saw in Genesis, sin is first a violation of our relationship with God—we mistrust His goodness. It is secondly a violation of our relationship with ourselves—we put ourselves on the throne instead of God. And it is lastly a violation of our relationships with other people—in our misguided attempt to be our own gods, we become selfish orphans who hurt others in many ways. Unraveling this pattern is a matter of repairing the relationships we've hurt in the same order. As I encourage in the Five Es, we must repent and be reconciled to God, then to ourselves, and then to others.

If we are waiting for someone to clean up a mess with us, it's important to pray, hope, and expect that the person is first cleaning up their mess and reconciling with God and themselves. Creating space for this allows them to walk out a degree of repentance that will convince us that they are actually going to change—it's how they will come to us able to say, "I found the problem and here's what I'm doing to fix it." Reconciliation is the opportunity that repentance creates. It's also important to understand what reconciliation is and how it works.

WHAT IS RECONCILIATION?

Many people think that reconciling with someone means putting them back in a position of trust without seeing any sign that they have changed. And in the punishment paradigm, this is the only thing reconciliation can mean, because people don't change. So, what happens is, after the mess-maker has confessed and apologized and paid penance or jumped through whatever hoops we required of them, we decide if we want to reinstate their relationship. Often, we never trust them to hold their former position in our lives. If we do decide to trust them, it's because we are actively choosing to sweep the mess under the rug and act like it never happened. But nothing they or we do has actually cleaned up the mess. Typically, the reinstated relationship is filled with more shame, anxiety, and control, which only makes future messes inevitable. The punishment paradigm simply cannot reconcile or restore relationships.

In the new covenant, however, reconciliation and restoration become possible through the combination of forgiveness and repentance, which produces transformation. This is why the Bible describes reconciliation not as a matter of patching up an old relationship with the same old people in it, but of building a new relationship with new people in it. Consider Paul's famous passage on reconciliation in 2 Corinthians:

> Therefore, if anyone is in Christ, the new creation has come: The old has gone, the new is here! All this is from God, who reconciled us to himself through Christ and gave us the ministry of reconciliation: that God was reconciling the world to himself in Christ, not counting people's sins against them. And he has committed to us the message of reconciliation. We are therefore Christ's ambassadors, as though God were making his appeal through us. We implore you on Christ's behalf: Be reconciled to God. God made him who had no sin to be sin for us, so that in him we might become the righteousness of God. (2 Corinthians 5:17-21)

This statement is packed with the language of *exchange*. The Greek word for reconciliation means to "change . . . coins for others of equivalent value."[16] God forgives us by removing our sin from our account and putting it on Jesus. He takes Jesus' righteousness from His account and gives it to us. By doing this, He exchanges the old creation for the new creation, and our old relationship with Him for a brand-new relationship. In the process, He reveals His profound value for us—He treats us as having equivalent value to Him!

Reconciling our relationship with God is a matter of entering into the finished work of reconciliation He has already accomplished through the cross. The great rift between God and humanity was settled between Jesus and the Father 2,000 years ago. "While we were still enemies, God fully reconciled us to himself through the death of his Son" (Romans 5:10

---

[16] "G2643 - katallagē - Strong's Greek Lexicon (NIV)." Blue Letter Bible. Accessed 14 Jul, 2019. https://www.blueletterbible.org//lang/lexicon/lexicon.cfm?Strongs=G2643&t=NIV

TPT). It is an incredible thing to know that when we repent for our sin, we don't have to wonder whether the Father will respond with forgiveness—He already has! His entire goal since the fall has been restoring our relationship with Him, which then restores our relationships with ourselves, others, and all of creation. All we do is receive His reconciliation with us as a gift and enter into it by faith.

Reconciling with our Father initiates us into reconciliation with ourselves. Through repentance and forgiveness, we journey from who we were in the punishment paradigm to who we are in Christ, exchanging the old shame-based belief in our unworthiness for the new truth of our value in Him, the orphan identity for that of a son or daughter, a heart of stone for a heart of flesh, and the spirit of fear for the spirit of power, love, and a sound mind.

Reconciling with the Father and ourselves enables us to reconcile with others—to exchange our old relationships for new relationships. Reconciliation means trading in the fear-fueled connections of orphans for love-fueled connections of sons and daughters. At their core, orphan relationships are the agreement of two self-preservationists to use one another to meet their own needs. New covenant relationships are the agreement of sons and daughters to lay down their lives in self-giving love to meet one another's needs. Repentance and forgiveness enable us to break our old agreements and form new agreements. That is reconciliation.

FORGIVENESS AND SOUL TIES

The miracle that couple experienced in my office demonstrates the critical power of forgiveness in the reconciliation process. Both husband and wife had to forgive to step into the miracle—the husband had to forgive his father, and the wife had to forgive her husband.

The broken spot in the husband's life came from a father wound, a mess that was never cleaned up. Because there was no repentance or forgiveness in that situation, the husband remained a victim of his father's sin, which ultimately led him to victimize his wife and family. This is how sin and punishment cycle through people, relationships, families, communities, generations, and cultures. Victims become the victimizers and reproduce themselves in others.

Forgiveness is the only thing that interrupts this cycle of victimization. The lie we believe in the punishment paradigm is that to forgive means saying that someone's sin wasn't wrong or removing all the consequences for their poor choices. In reality, forgiveness says, "What you did was wrong, but I am not going to respond with punishment. I am neither your judge nor your punisher. We both stand accountable to God for our sins. He offers us full and free forgiveness, and on that basis, I extend the same to you. Yes, there are consequences that need to be walked through to clean up this mess, but my heart toward you is not to see you punished but restored."

By forgiving instead of punishing, we break our agreement with the punishment paradigm and align ourselves with the new covenant, which allows the grace of reconciliation and restoration to flow into our lives. As soon as that man forgave his father, his bondage to sin was broken, and he received a transforming download of healing and truth. His wife then stopped the cycle of victimization on her side by forgiving her husband, opening the door for her to receive a download of trust and love. Through forgiveness, they severed their ties with the relational culture of fear, exchanged it for a new culture of love, and a brand-new connection was born. Or, to use a term from inner healing and deliverance ministry, they received grace for broken and unhealthy soul ties to be cleansed and healed.

One of the primary goals of the reconciliation and restoration process is to heal broken soul ties. Soul ties are emotional and spiritual bonds that exist in all our significant relationships—including our relationships with God and ourselves. When people bonded by love, marriage, or trust break their relationship, they do not just become whole again automatically. Imagine boards that are laminated together like a piece of plywood. If that plywood is separated in an attempt to recreate the original individual boards, then you will see what the lamination process created: one piece of wood. Separation will be messy. There will be pieces of one board torn apart from the original and now stuck to the other. The bond of the glue will not allow the plywood to separate cleanly. Soul ties work in a similar fashion. Forgiveness and a process of "binding and loosing" is needed for each person to get back what walked away with the other person and releasing what does not belong to them. An example of such a "binding and loosing" prayer is, "I release myself from the accusations, blame, and shame of this divorce. I am not held hostage to my spouse's decisions or actions. I call back my innocence, peace, and wholeness, which are mine through forgiveness in Christ." Healing soul ties is possible whether the other person repents or not, and it is critical for forming a new, healthy bond with someone in reconciliation.

UNFORGIVENESS AND PUNISHMENT

While forgiveness removes punishment from our response to a mess, unforgiveness hangs on to punishment. Not forgiving is saying, "I am your judge and your punisher. I will make you pay for your crime." Unforgiveness keeps us trapped in the punishment paradigm just as surely as unrepentance. As I mentioned in Chapter 2, when I present the "unpunishable" approach to confronting someone in a mess, the first question many people ask is, "What if they don't repent?" Much less frequently do I hear the other, equally important question: "What if we don't forgive?" The answer is that if we don't forgive, we are living outside the new covenant. We are victims bound in the cycle of victimization, and it won't be long before our bitter judgment, anger, and shame spill over into us victimizing others.

This is exactly the picture Jesus paints in His parable about the servant who didn't forgive after being forgiven a great debt. At first glance, the punchline of this parable seems harsh:

> "In anger his master handed him over to the jailers to be tortured, until he should pay back all he owed. This is how my heavenly Father will treat each of you unless you forgive your brother or sister from your heart." (Matthew 18:34-35)

But remember, God's wrath and punishment are always a matter of Him removing His hand and honoring our sinful choices and their consequences. Jesus makes a point of showing that the servant never asks his master for forgiveness—he only asks for time to pay off his debt: "'Be patient with me,' he begged, 'and I will pay back everything'" (Matthew 18:26). Knowing that the servant has absolutely no hope of ever paying off such a great debt in his lifetime, the master offers him the unasked-for and undeserved gift of forgiveness. But when the forgiven servant throws a fellow servant in prison for saying, "Be patient with me, and I will pay it back" (Matthew 18:29), the master knows that the servant wants nothing to do with either receiving or giving forgiveness. He wants to operate in a relational culture of victims and victimizers, a culture where you either pay off your debt or go to prison—the punishment paradigm. In "handing him over to the jailers," the master is honoring his servant's choice not to enter the relational culture of forgiveness into which he invited him.

PRACTICING FORGIVENESS

Jesus' parable doesn't just show us the prison of punishment we end up in when we don't forgive, however. It points the way to embracing the practice of forgiveness in our lives. Like everything in the kingdom, forgiveness is something we can only give by first receiving it for ourselves. The master in the parable expected his servant to forgive because he expected his heart to be changed by the experience of receiving forgiveness. We know we have comprehended the mercy and love of God towards us when it absolutely wrecks our hearts and fills them with gratitude, joy, humility, and total surrender. These reformed hearts will be delightedly honored to show fellow humans the small mercy of forgiving their offenses toward us after being forgiven the great offense of our own sin by God. Those forgiven much, love much (see Luke 7:47).

Whenever we find ourselves struggling to forgive, we need to recognize that our issue is first and foremost between us and God. Something is missing in our perception of His heart and the magnitude of what He has done to demonstrate His sacrificial love for us and save us from punishment. We haven't truly comprehended or received the reality of these things in a way that changes our hearts. Almost always, our struggle is rooted in the old orphan mistrust that He is good and just. To receive His forgiveness and become capable of forgiving "from our hearts" as our Father expects, we must repent for this mistrust by identifying the lies we have believed and replacing them with truth that enables us to trust Him fully.

In this repentance process, many of us may need to walk through forgiving God. In principle, we know God does nothing that needs to be forgiven. However, it is quite possible for us to have judgments in our hearts towards God, usually for allowing bad things to happen in our lives or the world. We use these judgments as grounds to mistrust Him and put ourselves in His place as the judge and punisher. Forgiving Him means repenting for believing the lie that He is not good or just, releasing Him from our undeserved judgments and punishments, stepping off the throne, and realigning our hearts to trust Him to be the good and just God He truly is.

Sometimes our struggle is with forgiving ourselves—something we must all do in the process of repentance and reconciliation. Many people live in a prison of self-condemnation and self-hatred because they cannot forgive themselves for something they did or didn't do. In order to escape from this prison, they must take the same path of humility and surrender and recognize that they are putting themselves in the place of God. Who are they to condemn themselves when the Father offers them free and full forgiveness? To forgive themselves, they must step off the throne of judgment and allow Him to be the righteous judge.

The same truth applies when struggling to forgive another person. Classically, the experience of being victimized by another person's mess leaves us feeling powerless. Their sin and the pain it caused can appear more powerful than God's love, justice, and ability to restore. When we believe this lie, we place those who have victimized us on the throne instead of God. To forgive them, we must repent for making them more powerful than God in our lives and recognize the truth of His superior power and authority.

JONATHAN'S RECONCILIATION JOURNEY

When I reached the Exploration step of the Five Es with Jonathan and asked him, "Who has been affected by this mess?" I remember being the one to point out that God should be first on his list. This respected theologian and expert on the Better Covenant couldn't yet see that his core problem—his terror of being destroyed—had produced a massive disconnect between him and the Father. He was not trusting God to protect him from destruction. He was trusting himself, as evidenced by his self-preservationist strategy of building his life and ministry into a "castle" of control. This broken trust with the Father was the first mess he needed to address on his reconciliation journey.

Trust in every relationship is built through the exchange of truth. The Jonathan I initially encountered in the confrontation process consistently lied and denied when presented with the truth, which told me that he had to also be lying and denying to himself and to God. (This is the case with everyone who ends up in a hot mess.) Once he realized he was boxed in, however, he stopped running, changed course, began to listen to what he was hearing, and started searching for the truth. When we finally struck gold by identifying his core fear of being destroyed, he began to taste hope that the truth would actually set him free. I urged and challenged him that his next step was to take this fear to God and work on getting more honest with the Father and himself than ever before.

Jon did just that. With the help of his counselor and other inner healing resources, he began to confront the lies he had believed, trace them back to the broken spot in his life, walk through forgiveness and repentance to receive the truth, and began planting that truth in his heart and mind. As it turned out, the hardest part of the reconciliation process was Jon reconciling with himself. His counselor told him that his inability to forgive himself was unlike anybody he had ever worked with in twenty years of professional counseling. They devoted three whole sessions to discussing the topic before Jon was willing to begin forgiving himself. Once he gave himself permission to let himself off the chopping block, days and days of weeping and forgiving himself followed. These putrid layers of unforgiveness toward himself had created all the shame, hiding, and self-hatred. In the process, like the prodigal son, he remembered the Father and his true identity, and recognized the distortion through which he had been viewing the Father and himself for so many years. As he broke his agreements with this old identity and relationship, he was free to align his heart and mind with the truth of who his Father truly was and how He saw him as His son. This process of exchange didn't happen overnight, but with every step along the way he moved deeper into the experience of reconciliation with God and with himself.

The next person with whom Jon needed to clean up his mess was Karen. As I mentioned, she had instituted a ninety-day separation agreement to communicate to Jon that both he and their relationship had to change. She knew that if Jonathan continued with his behavior, it would destroy their marriage and family. However, she had hope. Before she knew everything that was going on, she had received a promise from God that this season would produce the husband she had always prayed for. When the truth came to light, she leaned on this promise for the courage to set the necessary limits with her husband so the Holy Spirit could do His job of transforming Jon and their relationship.

Karen told me that the months of the separation were the most difficult time of her life. She was eight months pregnant when she learned the full truth of Jonathan's betrayal, and was immediately thrust into survival mode trying to manage the closing of the school, take care of two little kids, and plan for the birth of her daughter. She could have made her life easier in the short term by letting Jon come home before he had at least found the problem and started to work on it. But she held the line, and in doing so created leverage that motivated her husband to dig into the process of repenting and reconciling with God and himself.

Early on in the separation, Karen cut off communication with Jonathan completely because he was so angry and unstable. She also made the very difficult decision that he would not be welcome at the birth of their daughter until he made some serious changes. Gradually, she resumed limited communication with him and was able to see that he was working hard to get healing and try to figure out how to repent.

"I was still skeptical because I had been fooled in the past," she told me. "Jonathan is so smart at figuring out what the 'right answer' should be and can convince himself and everyone else that he's got it. But I didn't trust him, and I didn't even trust myself to see him clearly. I trusted your perspective, Danny, more than my own during this time."

One of the difficulties Karen discussed with me was whether she ought to change her mind and allow her husband to attend the birth of their daughter, which was scheduled to take place in the middle of the separation. She explained that as a doula, and having experienced peaceful, pain-free, "supernatural" childbirth with her first two babies, she knew her body needed to feel totally safe and protected in order to labor effectively. She didn't know if she could feel safe to be vulnerable enough to take her walls down with Jonathan there or trust him to support her. On the other hand, her husband's absence at the birth would be traumatizing in its own way. She was hoping and believing that God could do a miracle and bring about enough transformation in Jon by the time of the birth so she could feel safe with him. At the same time, she was wary about opening her heart too early and surrendering the leverage she'd created with the separation to require adjustment from Jon.

"Do you think it's possible for me to open my heart and then close it again?" Karen asked me.

"I think it is," I said. "I think you just need to be really clear in communicating to Jonathan what you need from him to feel safe—at the birth and in your new relationship." I then gave her a series of questions to ask herself before, during, and after her conversation with Jonathan:

- Do you know what you need to feel?
- Did you tell him that?
- What was his response?
- Did you believe him?
- How did it feel when you listened to his response?
- What feels familiar?
- What feels new?

Days before her delivery, Karen spoke with Jonathan and clearly communicated what she needed from him for her to feel good about having him at the birth. "I need to feel safe, cared for, and protected in your presence," she told him. "I need to feel like I am your highest priority and focus. I cannot have you bring anxiety, stress, and fear into the room. I need you to step up and man up if you want to be present for the birth of our daughter."

Jonathan rose to the occasion and supported Karen through her labor. She told me that he did a great job at setting aside all the issues he was dealing with and being present, emotionally available, and connected with her in a way she had never experienced. She was able to accept him and where he was in his healing process. The birth took place in intimacy, safety, and peace, and even the birth attendants commented on the presence of God in the room.

After the birth, Karen continued with the separation, well aware that they still had a lot of work to do before they would be ready to reconcile. But something had shifted for both of them through that experience. Jonathan returned to his own repentance and healing work, and Karen to caring for her newborn and pursuing her own healing. A couple months later, when the ninety days were up, I got on the phone with them for a progress report. It was clear that they had both made significant strides in repentance and forgiveness, and their hearts were both pointed at one another with the goal of connection. I gave my support to them resuming their marriage and continuing to work on their reconciliation under the same roof.

The next relationships with "paint" on them were Jonathan's leaders and ministry colleagues. Most of these people had agreed to be on the newly formed advisory board that was providing accountability and oversight in his restoration process. Jon scheduled calls with most of these leaders to ask for forgiveness, update them on the work he was doing to fix the problem, and ask what he needed to be doing to clean up his mess with them.

He had gotten through most of these calls, which all went well, when we held a video conference call for Jonathan and Karen to update the board on how the marriage reconciliation was going. Everyone expressed joy and gratitude to hear about the healing they were experiencing individually and together. Then the conversation shifted and one of the leaders—with whom Jon had not yet had a one-on-one "clean up the mess" conversation—asked him a pointed question about whether he'd uncovered the reasons for his bad behavior toward his staff members. I watched Jonathan start to freeze up and get defensive as he struggled to answer. His fear reaction continued through the rest of the conversation, which did not end well, and for several weeks after that I heard only radio silence from Jonathan. When we finally got a chance to debrief, he explained that the conversation had exposed the fear dynamic he had always had in his relationship with that particular friend, as well as another person on the board. After the work he had done to uproot his fear of destruction, he had been surprised to see it raise its head in that moment. But he had done what he needed to do—he took the issue to his counselor and to the Lord and again broke his agreements with fear, specifically in those friendships. He then went back to his friends, was vulnerable about the fear issues that had always plagued their relationships, and invited them to step into reconciliation by finding a way to shift the dynamic from fear to love and a safe connection.

AN IMPORTANT ROLE OF LEADERSHIP IN THE RECONCILIATION PROCESS

As of this writing, Jonathan's next step is cleaning up his mess with his staff members, which he is preparing to do. Early in his restoration journey, I communicated with this group and asked, "If I bring a repentant Jonathan to you, would you want to talk to him?" Every one of them said, "Yes." Their heart was not to see him punished or destroyed but healed and restored. They wanted to forgive him. However, some of them had questions about what reconciliation with Jonathan would involve. They seemed to think that my expectation was that they would all be close friends on the other side of this, which concerned them.

"The reason you had this relationship with Jonathan was because you worked for him, and that will not be happening again," I responded. "What reconciliation looks like for you is that there is no residue of Jonathan's mess sticking to either of you as you move forward. My goal is that every time you hear his name, have a memory, or enjoy the 'Better Covenant,' there's no anxiety or sense that you need to protect yourself or others from him. Instead, you think, 'I love that guy.' And when you move on to your next job and relationship with a leader, I want you to bring your whole heart with you."

Reconciling—exchanging an old relationship for a new relationship—does not mean that the new relationship will have the same roles or level of closeness as the old one. A dating couple who makes a mess by having sex before marriage may clean up their mess by repenting and forgiving one another, yet ultimately decide that their reconciled relationship will not be a dating relationship. Or, an employer who removes an employee for irresponsibility or incompetence won't necessarily decide to rehire them simply because she has forgiven them and is willing to be friendly with them socially. The beauty of reconciliation is that these relational adjustments, though usually painful, are healthy and beneficial to everyone involved. What makes the reconciliation successful is that both parties are committed to fully cleaning up the mess through repentance and forgiveness, and forming a relationship on the other side that is free of fear and full of love and honor, whatever its level of contact or intimacy.

In providing leadership and accountability in a reconciliation process, my role is not to help people chart a path back to roles and relationships they had before the mess. Instead, I am there to help them clarify what healthy relationships will look like after the mess and determine when they are ready to move forward with each successive level of reconciliation. Here, one of my biggest responsibilities is discerning when we have "neutralized the threat"—that is, when the person cleaning up their mess has advanced sufficiently in their process of repentance to step into reconciliation. In Jonathan's case, this meant walking with him closely enough to be able to confirm to Karen, the advisory board, and the staff members that he is safe enough to return to the relationship and has a solid foundation of understanding for how those relationships need to adjust moving forward.

In my experience, some of the people who need the most assurance and help to see a repentant person are the leaders in the environment where the person made the mess—especially church leaders. As a church leader myself, I understand this need very well. Our job as shepherds is to protect innocent people from harm. Like parents, we feel responsible if one of our "kids" gets hurt on our watch, so when we perceive a threat, we confront and extract it as quickly as we can. However, we must remember that the mess-maker is also one of our "kids." When leaders err on the side of protecting the group against the mess-maker without being able to see that the person in repenting, they can end up punishing the mess-maker and cutting them off from reconciliation.

I watched this very thing unfold in another discipline process with a dear friend of mine. This young woman, a lifelong, devoted believer who has always been active in ministry, shocked herself and everyone who knew her when she admitted that one of her close friendships with another young woman had become emotionally addictive and sexually immoral. At first, she tried to minimize the situation, manage her behavior, and cling to this inappropriate relationship. But this only caused the mess to grow and spill out on her family, close friends, roommates, church leadership, and church community. Finally, through confrontations with me and others, she saw the truth of what was happening, admitted she needed help, ended the relationship, found the problem that had led to this behavior, and began the journey of repentance and reconciliation. I provided oversight and accountability for her, along with several other leaders. She did an incredible job of going after inner healing and stepping into reconciliation conversations with the people she had scared and broken trust with. Everyone forgave her and was thrilled to see her step toward becoming the best version of herself.

However, when my friend began to interact with church leaders who weren't involved in her restoration, but had seen and dealt with the impact of her mess at some level, it was not a fun experience. They clearly still perceived her as a threat to the environment. For close to a year after her repentance, my friend felt punished by these leaders. After doing everything asked of her to clean up her mess, she still felt excluded, judged, and ostracized by those she had trusted to love and protect her. As a result, she felt cut off from the opportunity to step into full reconciliation with them and people in the community as she desired.

Thankfully, my friend chose to keep her love on and be patient in winning the trust of her leaders. We set up a meeting with her leaders in which I explained that she was no longer a threat and should be allowed to reconcile and participate fully in relationships with people in the community. My friend was also vulnerable about her pain in feeling punished and her desire to be restored. Their perspective has shifted now, and they are able to see how she is becoming healthier than ever in her repentance journey. I'm proud of my friend for sticking with the process, choosing to pursue connection, and not getting offended or walking away while waiting for others to reciprocate. This tenacity in the reconciliation process is what paves the way for full restoration.

CHAPTER 10
RESTORATION

When Jonathan shared the story of the restoration process he had walked through following his infidelity early in his marriage, he told me that one of the leaders in his apostolic network had commented, "Yours is one of the best stories of restoration we've seen in this ministry." But of course, he hadn't really been restored, because he had never really repented. The leader to whom he was accountable in that restoration process had encouraged him to work on his identity as a son and his connection with the Father, which was a step in the right direction, but didn't really walk closely enough with him to make sure he had found and fixed the broken spot. As a result, Jonathan only dealt with the symptoms of his behavior.

It's so tempting to be satisfied by good behavior after a mess. Parents love it when their kids stop misbehaving and start cleaning their rooms, getting good grades, and being respectful. Husbands and wives love it when their spouse apologizes and starts performing better as a domestic and romantic partner. Leaders love it when their teams stop underperforming and start executing their tasks and hitting their goals. Pastors love it when their people clean up their acts and start coming to church regularly, going to Bible study, and volunteering to serve. It's tempting for the mess-maker to be satisfied too. *I've done everything they asked me to do,* they reason. *I've confessed and apologized profusely. I've complied with their demands. I took my punishment and I punished myself for good measure. I stopped sinning and have been keeping a good record ever since. Surely, I am restored.*

It's tempting to be satisfied because short-term behavior change is easier than long-term heart transformation. But Jonathan, Ben, and so many others show us what happens when we try to adjust our outsides without finding and fixing the broken spot on the inside. Apologizing, beating ourselves up, vowing to change, and working hard to behave actually distract us from looking at that root system of beliefs and motives. If we end up being successful at keeping up a front of good behavior for a long time, we step into a greater level of self-deception that we've dealt with the problem, allowing that root system to grow unchecked, until we're shocked to find ourselves in the same—now bigger—hole as before.

The world is satisfied with behavior modification because that's the best humans can do to restore ourselves without the gospel. As members of the body of Christ, however, we cannot be satisfied by worldly restoration. God's not satisfied by it, and He has paid the ultimate price to bring us into true, radical restoration from the inside out. This is the whole purpose and hope of the new covenant.

BECOMING WHO WE OUGHT TO BE

When Paul instructed us to "restore" those caught in sin (Galatians 6:1), he used a Greek word that means "to complete thoroughly" or "to make one what he ought to be."[17] The idea is not to put someone back into the condition they were before they sinned, but to bring them into wholeness and maturity according to their divine design.

---

[17] "G2675 - katartizō - Strong's Greek Lexicon (NIV)." Blue Letter Bible. Accessed 18 Jul, 2019. https://www.blueletterbible.org//lang/lexicon/lexicon.cfm?Strongs=G2675&t=NIV

When we look at the grand narrative of Scripture, this is the overarching theme. The gospel is not a story about God redeeming humanity by taking us back to the garden before sin entered the world. The humans in the garden—untested and easily deceived—were not the spiritually mature, wise sons and daughters we are designed to be. They were ready to believe lies about the Father, to imagine that He was withholding good things from them, and that they were capable of ruling and reigning apart from Him.

The humans we are meant to be look like Jesus Christ. In Him we see two great truths about how the Father "makes us who we ought to be." First, though He Himself never sinned, Jesus demonstrated that the Father's heart is not to punish His sinful children, but to *meet us in our sin* with forgiveness and reconciliation. He doesn't want to punish our mistrust and rebellion—He wants to teach us the truth of His trustworthiness, love, and faithfulness. He wants us to see how idolatry only leads to spiritual exile, orphanhood, slavery, despair, and destruction, while setting Him on the throne of our hearts brings us home to the place of belonging where we were created to flourish as His beloved children. The way He does this is by pursuing us to the utter extreme of our attempt to run from Him—becoming one of us, putting on our flesh, suffering our temptations, and walking through our death. This is how He tells us, "I love you. I am not withholding anything good from you. All that I have, all that I am, is yours for eternity. Even when you are faithless, I am faithful. Even when you believe lies about me, I keep pursuing you with the truth of my love. Nothing you have done has changed my love for you. You were made for my love. You can trust me. Stop running, and come home to my arms."

I like to imagine the way this truth plays out in our lives as a line on a graph. When we say yes to following Jesus, that line begins to ascend, representing our growth in connection with Him, ourselves, and others. When we sin, the line takes a dip. For those of us who end up in a "hot mess," that dip looks like a pretty deep valley. But the lowest point—the point of repentance—is where God meets us with a revelation of His great love and forgiveness that confronts and casts out fear and shame. This encounter with perfect love is what sets us on an ascending path of restoration that doesn't just bring us back to the level of trust and connection we had before our decline, but to a much greater level, so that it looks like we've ended up where we were heading before the crash.

The second truth is that in Jesus, we see what it looks like to be those mature sons and daughters who trust their Father and walk in His perfect love. One of the best words to describe the reality in which Jesus lived is *shalom*. We typically translate this word as "peace," but miss its richness because we think of peace as calmness, serenity, and the absence of conflict. *Shalom* is relational wholeness. It's living in loving connection with God, ourselves, others, and creation as we were designed, which produces safety, health, happiness, and prosperity.[18]

As Jesus demonstrated, living in *shalom* is incredibly powerful. It enabled Him to speak a word in the midst of a life-threatening storm and restore divine order. Brian Simmons explains this restorative power of *shalom* in one of his notes in *The Passion Translation*:

> [*Shalom*] means much more than peace. It means wholeness, wellness, well-being, safe, happy, friendly, favor, completeness, to make peace, peace offering, secure, to prosper, to be victorious, to be content, tranquil, quiet, and restful. The pictographic symbols for the word *shalom* (*shin, lamed, vav, mem*) read "Destroy the authority that binds to chaos." The noun *shalom* is derived from the verbal root *shalam*, which means "to restore,"

[18] "H7965 - shalowm - Strong's Hebrew Lexicon (NIV)." Blue Letter Bible. Accessed 19 Jul, 2019. https://www.blueletterbible.org//lang/lexicon/lexicon.cfm?Strongs=H7965&t=NIV

> in the sense of replacing or providing what is needed in order to make someone or something whole and complete. So *shalom* is used to describe those of us who have been provided all that is needed to be whole and complete and break off all authority that would attempt to bind us to chaos.[19]

Chaos is what we experience living outside of divine order and relational wholeness, disconnected from God, our own hearts, and others. Stepping outside of divine order and violating our relationships gives the enemy access to use his spiritual power—fear—to keep us in bondage. Because Jesus lived in *shalom*, He carried the power and authority to *shalom* others—to break the enemy's power and bring them into wholeness. This is what He is doing in our lives. As we walk with Him, He confronts everything out of order, broken, or lacking and brings it into divine order. As we see in the Gospels, He starts with restoring specific problems of body, mind, and spirit—sickness, infirmity, demonic torment, and sin. But these breakthroughs are not full restoration—they are invitations to be fully restored at the deepest level in our ability to walk, as He does, in unbroken trust and connection with the Father, ourselves, and others. He is restoring us to live in *shalom* and to *shalom* others just as He does.

WHAT DOES RESTORATION LOOK LIKE?

In another conversation with Jonathan and Karen, I asked them, "What does restoration look like for you? What is the future you are building with God and each other that you want to live in?"

Jonathan began to describe some of the things he was beginning to experience as he allowed the Father to dismantle his core fear of being destroyed. He recounted a morning where he sat down with his Bible

[19] The Passion Translation, footnote to Psalm 34:14.

and found that he actually wanted to read it, not to help him write his next book or increase his knowledge, but just to connect with God. "I began to read Galatians 4 where it talks about the spirit in us crying out and making us heirs to sonship, and for the first time in my life I realized that my heart was connecting with this reality," he told me. "For years it had been a concept in my head. I had tried to perform for it and be perfect enough, but couldn't ever receive the truth that He accepts me. Now I was finally starting to believe in my heart that I am a son. I am loved."

He said that the same heart connection was beginning to affect the way he was showing up in relationships. "I've always walled people out and called it 'setting boundaries,'" he admitted. "I've pushed people away and cut them off in the name of keeping my relationships 'safe.' But it was all driven by this core fear, not from being powerful and valuing myself and the other person. I didn't value myself. Now I'm finally starting to accept my feelings and let other people see them. I'm finally being vulnerable out of a place of wanting to be seen and heard, and trusting others to care for me and protect my heart."

"For me, restoration is really about living into this new lifestyle of connection. Everything shifted when I saw that I needed to give up the priority of self-protection, of walling myself off as the king of my castle, and make protecting connection my priority. So restoration for me is learning to live in relationships of authenticity, vulnerability, honesty, and openness."

Karen echoed her husband. "Living authentically is something I've always wanted," she said. "And for me that begins with our family. Right now, that's the restoration that's most important to me—to see our connection with each other and our kids grow strong and healthy. If we can build that integrity in our love and honor for each other, then any ministry God opens for us will be an overflow of that."

When I heard these responses, I thought, *They're on their way.* The first seeds of *shalom* are beginning to sprout in their lives. While I don't know all the steps ahead for them on this journey or all the choices they will make, I am confident that if they continue along this path of connection, we will see them back in ministry—a ministry that looks nothing like the one Jonathan built with his "king of the castle" relational culture. It will be built on the much stronger foundation of covenant love.

People are naturally wary about a fallen leader returning to a position of influence—especially once they find out that he is a repeat offender. However, often this wariness is an expression of the punishment paradigm. The reality is that many leaders today are repeat offenders without losing their position—they are just successful in hiding their sin or sinning in an "acceptable" way. For some reason, the sins of fear, anger, self-preservation, idolatry, gluttony, lust, and pride often get a pass in certain leaders. The sheer number of leaders regularly using porn in this present generation is staggering. But if we don't know about it, or we struggle with the same things ourselves, we continue to trust, empower, and follow these broken leaders. Then, when they crash and burn, we destroy them, even if they want to repent. When it comes to "restoring" them to a leadership position, our concern is not really to see whether they have learned to walk in a new relational culture of connection, vulnerability, and asking for help way before risking a crash, but whether they have learned their lesson about keeping their sin tucked in. This only enforces the message to other leaders who are struggling that it's not safe to be vulnerable, ask for help, and repent before they finally blow some part of their lives apart. In the new covenant, however, our priority should be to appoint leaders who are healthy enough to ask for the help they need, while continuing in the leadership gift they are to the body of Christ. In my experience, some of the leaders who know the most about being healthy are those who have been restored after repenting for their sin.

If a leader has not repented, then I am skeptical about trusting them anywhere near a leadership role until they do. But when they repent, I expect God to restore them—as people and as leaders—because that is what He does. He did it with Ben and Heather. The relational culture they live in now looks nothing like what they had before Ben repented. The isolation, shame, and disconnection that had been hiding in both of their lives is gone. They have built a new normal of letting their hearts be seen and living in connection. The minute they get scared, they have a default of self-awareness to check that and lean into the strength of their connections. If they don't—if they allow the fear to lead them into retreating from vulnerability and connection, the people around them take notice and call them on it: "Hey, where are you? I can't see you. I feel disconnected from you. Where'd you go?" Building this culture of connection has filled their marriage, family, and ministry with *shalom*, and they are walking in authority to bring the *shalom* they live in to everyone around them. Their position of leadership in people's lives is the fruit of the believability of their transformation. People trust them. I hope and expect nothing less to be the case for Jonathan and Karen. My goal in sharing their story, which is very much still in process, is to invite you into that same hope and expectation—for them and for everyone on the journey of repentance, reconciliation, and restoration.

RESTORING PAULS

It's easy to forget that most of the New Testament was written by a man Jesus restored. Before Jesus encountered Saul on the road to Damascus, Saul was a religious terrorist on a mission to murder Christians. He was the church's public enemy number one. After his encounter, he became one of its greatest champions. Imagine Osama bin Laden becoming President of the United States—that's how drastic it was for Saul the Pharisee to become Paul the apostle. His dramatic transformation shows us several important keys to understanding how Jesus restores us.

First, when Jesus restored Paul, He didn't just "neutralize the threat." He made Saul what he was always meant to be. He was the Pharisee of Pharisees, "advancing in Judaism beyond many of [his] own age . . . extremely zealous for the traditions of [his] fathers" (Galatians 1:14). His repentance and conversion did not dim this zeal—it simply attached it to a new motive and a new goal. Instead of punishing lawbreakers, Paul began to build up sons and daughters.

This is the pattern I see played out in everyone who is restored. Ben Armstrong always wanted and was designed to be a loving husband, father, and pastor. Sin caused him to fail in those roles and betray those relationships. Yet the restoration Christ has brought about in his life has caused him to become the husband, father, and pastor he was meant to be. Likewise, Jonathan has always carried the desire to walk in sonship and equip people to walk in the reality of the "Better Covenant." The full restoration awaiting him through this journey of repentance and reconciliation is that he will do these things with greater integrity, authority, and power than ever before.

Second, Paul was not only restored—he became a restorer. That is, walking through his own discipline journey birthed passion and authority to lead others in the same journey. One thing that stands out about the letters of Paul is that they are full of confrontation and correction. After being corrected and disciplined by Jesus Himself, Paul did not sit back and say, "As a former murderer and one who 'tried to destroy' the church (Galatians 1:13), I really don't have the authority to bring correction to anyone." The opposite seems to be the case. Paul was fearless about stepping into messes with people. He was not interested in saving face and pretending that the churches under his care had it all together. He also had no compunction about confronting other leaders for their hypocrisy—he even had the courage to correct Peter to his face for being a racist (Galatians 2:11). Paul's journey of being lovingly set right by Jesus was precisely what equipped him to discipline the churches he oversaw. Even when he had to recommend tough consequences, such as handing over an unrepentant man to Satan "for the destruction of the flesh," it was done in the hope that "his spirit may be saved on the day of the Lord" (1 Corinthians 5:5), and communicated with "great distress and anguish of heart and with many tears, not to grieve . . . but to let [them] know the depth of [his] love" (2 Corinthians 2:4). Paul displayed the Father's heart to bring His sons and daughters into divine order and relational wholeness.

Lastly, Acts 9 also shows that there were two key players in Paul's restoration process. The first was Ananias, whom Jesus instructed to go to Saul as he sat praying and blind immediately after his conversion. Imagine being told to go and see a notorious murderer of Christians with no evidence that he has changed. Ananias's courage and trust to obey Christ's words were remarkable. The second player was Barnabas, who took Paul before the apostles in Jerusalem and gave them his word that Paul was no longer a threat, but had been truly converted and was now a genuine disciple of Jesus. Ananias risked his own life by facing Paul, but Barnabas risked many lives by bringing a former murderer into the church—an even greater act of courage and trust that Paul's restoration was genuine. Both players paved the way for Paul to step freely into his new ministry as a preacher of the gospel.

In the kingdom, the greatest mess-makers are restored to become the greatest restorers. The "chief of sinners" is the one who receives the greatest revelation of the love of God and writes 1 Corinthians 13. This is the message of Paul's life, and the lives of so many others who have walked the journey of repentance, reconciliation, and restoration. But if we want to see more Pauls be restored, we need more men and women like Ananias and Barnabas—people who will step into the middle of a mess, discern that Jesus is at work, and walk alongside people on their journey. The body of Christ desperately needs spiritual fathers and mothers who, instead of punishing or being afraid of mistakes, break the shame from people's lives by moving toward them and saying, "What are you going to do? Let's grow through this. Let's figure out why you're doing this. Let's get into the heart. Let's get rid of the fear. Let's get connected to love. Let's get wholeness and peace happening here. Let's break off the entanglements of the past, the old models that were passed on to you from your parents. Let's forgive those who have hurt you. Let's get realigned with the kingdom and the Father's heart."

This is the perfect, mature love of Jesus in action. When this love is lacking, we allow the fear of punishment to become even more deeply embedded in people's hearts. One of the reasons why Ben and Jonathan ended up falling in the same hole twice was this: when they messed up the first time and no one invited them into the journey of repentance, it reinforced the lie that they weren't worthy of being restored. It amplified the orphan message that they were on their own to try to clean up the mess. In Jonathan's case, I believe one of the reasons he persisted in trying to protect himself through lying and denial was simply that he couldn't believe that someone would actually walk with him if he tried to face his mess and clean it up. After all, that's what happened before. Ironically, it was the experience of being boxed in and surrounded by a team of people who insisted, "No more lying, Jon—come into the light," that began to show him that he could finally wave the white flag as the lonely king of that castle and let people in whom he could trust to stay and help.

In one of my conversations with Karen, she said, "This season has been painful, but I see it as a gift, because this time we got to walk through this process with a team around us. We didn't have a team the first time. This time, I didn't have to be afraid, because I trusted this team. I trusted that they had our best interests at heart. I didn't have to try to control the process or worry about the outcome. I'm confident Jonathan would not have faced his pain and truly transformed without Danny's guidance, the team, and the work of Holy Spirit. God has restored our marriage and our family."

If we want a person who has made a mess to repent and convince us that their repentance is believable, then we need to convince them that our love is believable. This is what the Father did for us. He didn't wait for us to repent before showing us love and forgiveness. He showed us love, mercy, and forgiveness *to lead us* to repentance. This is the only way for us to lead others.

MAKING JESUS BELIEVABLE

Can you love someone and disagree with them? Can you love them and confront sin in their lives? These questions are hotly debated today. The answer to both is yes. Jesus did and does both all the time. So did Paul. Healthy confrontation of sin is actually an expression of mature love. But too often, this is not the experience we are creating in the body of Christ. We have been too busy, scared, ill-equipped, and immature to walk alongside people with healthy discipline.

Meanwhile, the world around us is desperate for a revelation of God's love. Too often, instead of encountering people who make His love believable to them, they see people spinning the illusion that the church is a mess-free organization, only to be exposed as hypocrites by the latest leadership crash. One of the reasons I am passionate about helping leaders like Ben and Jonathan repent and be restored is that I believe these are the very people who can help the body of Christ stop the pretense. This is the biblical model. Jesus chose Peter and Paul as the two primary fathers of the early church. Both were men who failed publicly and gladly owned up to that fact *in the Bible*. They did not pretend to have it all together. Instead they boasted in their weaknesses as the very places where Christ's love and power were perfected—became mature and complete—in their lives (2 Corinthians 12:9). The very fact that they failed and were disciplined and restored by Jesus caused people to trust them to put the Father's heart on display.

Some of Jesus' final words to His disciples before going to the cross, stepping into the utmost depths of our sinful mess, and taking our punishment were, "A new command I give you: Love one another. As I have loved you, so you must love one another. By this everyone will know that you are my disciples, if you love one another" (John 13:34-35). He followed this with His prayer to the Father:

> I pray for them all to be joined together as one
> even as you and I, Father, are joined together as one.
> I pray for them to become one with us
> so that the world will recognize that you sent me . . .
> You live fully in me and now I live fully in them
> so that they will experience perfect unity,
> and the world will be convinced that you have sent me,
> for they will see that you love each one of them
> with the same passionate love that you have for me. (John 17:20-21, 23 TPT)

It is our love for one another, our culture of connection and *shalom*, that makes Jesus believable to the world. The first and preeminent way we live out this love for one another is to follow Jesus' steps in confronting sin and its effects with sacrificial love and forgiveness. The church that is going to make Jesus' love believable is not just a church that moves in signs and wonders and bold gospel preaching and care for the poor. It is the church that has truly become a family. In a family, our mistakes and messes do not disqualify us from belonging—they expose just how deeply we belong. Every loving parent understands this. It's our kids messes that draw the greatest demonstrations of sacrificial love from our hearts and send the message, "Nothing can separate you from my love. No matter what you do, you are my child." This is the love that flows from leaders who have been delivered from the punishment paradigm and brought into the new covenant through their own journey of repentance, reconciliation, and restoration. These are the ones who mature to be true mothers and fathers who help turn orphans into sons and daughters.

The world around us is in a toxic love affair with punishment. Everywhere we look, people are wracked with anxiety, anger, and addictions as they struggle fruitlessly to find purpose, power, comfort, and safety without God. The only way for them to see that this love affair is not love at all, but absolute bondage to fear, sin, death, and hell, is for them to encounter the covenant of love between the Father and His children. This is the great privilege and honor of every restored son and daughter—to show the Father's lost children the punishment-free path back to His arms.

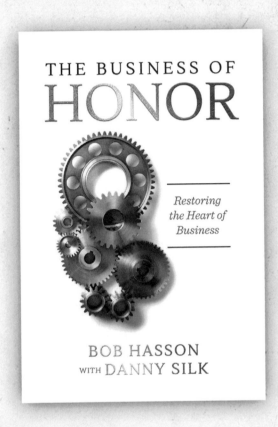

BUILDING CONNECTION, COMMUNICATING EFFECTIVELY, AND SETTING HEALTHY BOUNDARIES

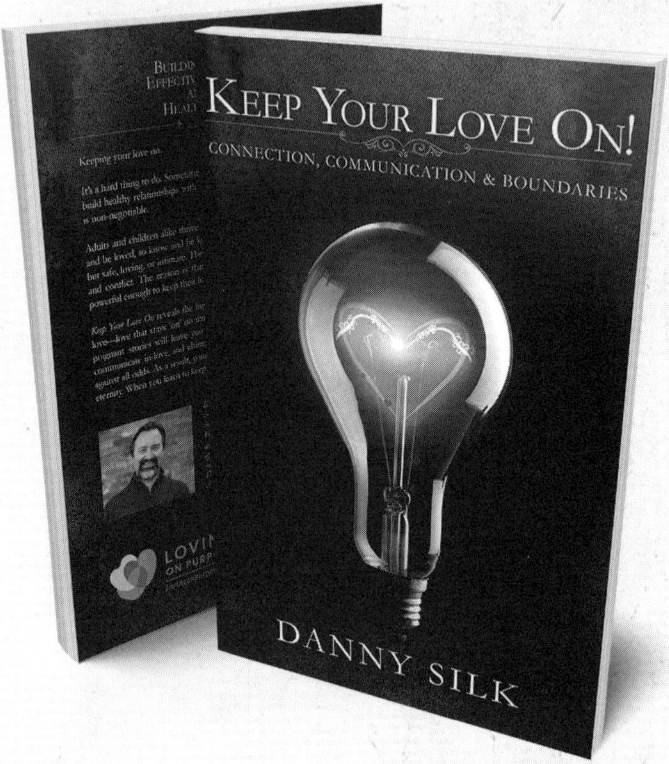

Keeping your love on is a hard thing to do. But if you want to build healthy relationships with God and others, learning to keep your love on is non-negotiable. *Keep Your Love On* reveals the higher, Jesus-focused standard defined by mature love—love that stays "on" no matter what. It will increase your power to draw healthy boundaries, communicate in love, and ultimately protect your connections so you can love against all odds. As a result, your relationships will be radically transformed for eternity. When you learn to keep your love on, you become like Jesus.

Visit this and more at Lovingonpurpose.com

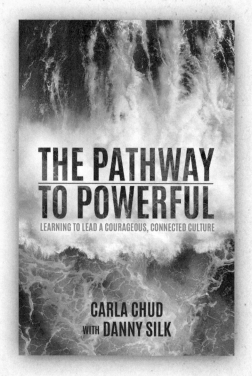